One Poultry speaks.

One Poultry
speaks.

Royal Institute of British Architects
Liverpool University Press

One Poultry Speaks, devised and edited by Marco Iuliano,
is a collaboration between the University of Liverpool,
whence James Stirling graduated in 1950,
and the Royal Institute of British Architects [RIBA],
which awarded him its Royal Gold Medal in 1980.

This publication accompanies the exhibition
Mies van der Rohe and James Stirling: Circling the Square,
curated by Marie Bak Mortensen and Vicky Wilson
at the RIBA Architectural Gallery, 8 March to 25 June 2017.

Special thanks to Laurence Bain, Alan Berman,
James Jones, Simon Nurney, François Penz,
Nicholas Ray and Michael Wilford.

Book layout by Luciano Striani

Cover image
Miniature radio in the shape of Number One Poultry, 1997,
acrylic; design Peter Murray, manufactured by Pipers Model,
photograph Nick Graham. The radio is based on a 1:500
model of the building and makes ironical reference to
Prince Charles's comment on Number One Poultry which,
in his view, looked like a wireless set of the 1930s.

Printed in Wales by Gomer Press
ISBN: 9781786940742

content

[Preface]

Number One Poultry, London EC2R 8EJ, was a commission awarded by Peter Palumbo to James Stirling, Michael Wilford and Associates in May 1985. Designed from July 1985 onwards, it was completed in 1998. This publication is divided into five sections not strictly linked to one another, therefore open to reading in several ways.

[Conversations] archives the dialogues between the building and five key interlocutors: these were recorded in February 2017 and are a truthful transcription of their words;

[Album] is a portfolio of sketches, drawings and photographs of the building from concept to realisation. Unless otherwise stated, all the materials are from Laurence Bain, project architect for One Poultry;

[Correspondence] contains a selection of letters sent by distinguished individuals to the City of London Planning Office. These letters protest against threatened alterations to One Poultry, highlighting the value of the building. Those interested in understanding the proposed modifications can consult the Planning Office archives;

[Listing] is the official document prepared by Historic England for the most recently constructed British architecture to have been listed. The document expands upon the Twentieth Century Society's campaign for the preservation of One Poultry - only 0.2% of all listed buildings date from the post-war period;

[Circling the Square] explores the history of the site, comparing the design methods of Mansion House Square and One Poultry.

Note to the Reader

The fact that buildings speak is well-known. We most frequently refer to the projects of the architects Étienne-Louis Boullée and Claude-Nicolas Ledoux, which their contemporaries considered an *architecture parlante*, "speaking architecture".[1] The most complete explanation that I have found to date on the subject comes from the filmmaker Wim Wenders in the presentation of his short documentary *If Buildings Could Talk*.[2] He writes:

> If Buildings Could Talk...
> some of them would sound like Shakespeare.
> Others would speak like the Financial Times,
> yet others would praise God, or Allah.
> Some would just whisper,
> some would loudly sing their own praises,
> while others would modestly mumble a few words
> and really have nothing to say.
> Some are plain dead and don't speak anymore...
> Buildings are like people, in fact.
> Old and young, male and female,
> ugly and beautiful, fat and skinny,
> ambitious and lazy, rich and poor,
> clinging to the past or reaching out to the future.
> Don't get me wrong: this is not a metaphor.
> Buildings do speak to us!
> They have messages. Of course.
> Some really want a constant dialogue with us.
> Some rather listen carefully first.
> And you have probably noticed:
> some of them like us a lot, some less and some not at all.
> Buildings, like people, are subject to time
> and exist in a three-dimensional world. [...]

On a number of different days during a mild winter in 2017, in London, I witnessed the conversations between One Poultry and those involved with it over its controversial lifetime. I was careful to hide whilst eavesdropping, so that they did not realise I was taking notes.

Lord Palumbo, developer and patron, was at the top floor window of *The Walbrook Club*, on a bright and crisp Sunday morning - when the City is fascinatingly silent. He was benefitting from the temporary emptiness of the Bloomberg headquarters building site, which gave him a partial, but clear view of the corner of One Poultry between Queen Victoria Street and Sise Lane. At twilight on a busy weekday, Michael Wilford, Jim's lifetime working partner, was sitting at a table in *The Green Man* - just inside Poultry's portico: there was some noise, so it was slightly difficult to hear the dialogue. While Laurence Bain, the project architect, with his definite voice, was chatting on Poultry's roof garden. I would have expected to observe Peter Rees there, the long standing City of London Planning Officer. During his conversation, instead, Peter was fascinated by the skin of the façades, admiring their alternating rows of stones. Finally, I saw Charles Jencks, the historian and architectural critic, engaged in a discussion I found very special, sitting on the steps of the *Scala Regia*, beyond the "keyhole" at the corner entrance. Poultry did not speak to me and unfortunately I never had the opportunity to witness Jim talking to his own creation. However, I heard Jim's voice in a compelling lecture recorded at the Architectural Association in 1982 and in a monographic documentary; I also gathered something of his thoughts through the people close to him, his notebook and via Bob Maxwell's collection of Jim's writings.[3]

Some could claim that in the following pages One Poultry is not properly speaking to people, rather it is asking questions. On this occasion, it might turn out to be true.

1. Emil Kaufmann, *Three Revolutionary Architects, Boullée, Ledoux and Lequeu,* (Philadelphia: American Philosophical Society, 1952) p. 441.
2. *If Buildings Could Talk*, directed by Wim Wenders (2010); the text herein quoted is Wender's own presentation of the movie - http://neueroadmovies.com.
3. The AA lecture is available on the School's web repository; the documentary is *Stirling*, directed by Michael Blackwood (1986). For the notebook see Mark Crinson (ed.), *James Stirling: Early Unpublished Writings on Architecture* (London: Routledge, 2009); Robert Maxwell, *James Stirling: Writings on Architecture* (Milan: Skira, 1998). My reflections on Jim's architecture are contained in Marco Iuliano and Francesca Serrazanetti (eds.), *James Stirling: Inspiration and Process in Architecture* (Milan: Moleskine, 2015).

[Conversations]

[with] Peter Palumbo

Why in the first place did you choose Mies for my unique, wedged site?

Mies was the obvious choice for me, because his mind-set was from northern Europe, he liked grey skies, he did not like sunshine so much. When I first saw him in 1962 one of the first things he asked me was: "Do you come from London?"
"Yes," I answered.
Mies replied: "Do you know the Berlage building in Bury Street? You should go and see it: it is a very good building."

So, when I got back to London, I went to Bury Street, St James's, West End, and I could not find any Berlage building. There was another Bury Street, which is here, in the City of London, and there it was. It was completed in 1916 for the Holland Steamship Company. A beautiful building, he was quite right. Mies said he was influenced by Berlage and so I should go and see it. He was in tune with northern skies, northern life and northern light, Mies. That was one reason. The other was I loved his architecture and I thought that it would be a welcome addition to this particular site, which is surrounded by interesting buildings. On the North side you have Edwin Lutyens, a neoclassical architect, with his Midland Bank building - a great building, I think - and then you have the Bank of England and two churches, one by Hawksmoor, who was one of Jim's heroes, and one by Wren, next door - beautiful interior, probably one of the greatest interiors, and also a prototype for the dome of St Paul's Cathedral. So you have a chronology, already, within 200 meters of one another, of very interesting buildings by extremely talented architects; and I thought that Mies could anchor the whole of the surroundings and have a conversation with them, not a confrontation, but a conversation, as an equal partner.

This came about because I had a wonderful art Master at Eton College, who was an artist himself and who had an encyclopedic knowledge of the arts. You cannot talk about art, you have to talk about the arts, because the arts are interdependent, they influence one another and you cannot just isolate, say architecture, poetry, film, painting, sculpture, dance, or whatever it is; you have to realise that they are all interdependent, there is a golden thread that links them together. That was lesson number one. Lesson number two was at a weekly seminar, which lasted one hour on a Sunday morning, after chapel and before lunch. He would discuss one artist with the senior boys - maybe 17 years old. One artist. First Jan van Eyck - we would do him, with photographs and talking about his life and times. The next Sunday we would do Jackson Pollock and then the question would be "What important characteristics do they have in common?" And then we would do Vermeer and Barnett Newman.

It was a wonderful awakening, really, to a dialogue that can be argued in so many ways, but for me it was a complete adventure - and eventually we did Palladio, and we did Mies.

It was the time when the Farnsworth house had just been built. I remember thinking I have never seen anything as beautiful as Farnsworth, in this sort of setting by the Fox River. By that time Corbu was dead, Frank Lloyd Wright had died in 1959, Alvar was dead, and Mies was the last of the great great architects - Louis Kahn had gone too.

I wrote to Mies saying we have an important site, not a huge site but at the epicentre of the city of London, Bank junction, half of a wheel, spoke of a wheel, and everything radiates from the Mansion House as a centre of civic authority; and the Bank of England, the

Stock Exchange and so on. It is important from the point of view of its location. So I said to my father, we should commission an architect who would be capable of making a contribution to the importance of the site. That must be Mies van der Rohe.

I went to see him, in Chicago. I was quite young, maybe 24 or something like that, and we got on very well because, as a fan, I knew his work, I knew his buildings from early on. I asked Mies: "Would you consider this? There is one condition attached: the building would not be built for 25 years." And that was because we did not own the whole site, we had 40% of it and we had to buy 60% of it. Although it is a small site it had many many interests, which we had to purchase one by one; hundreds leasehold interests, many of which go back to 14th century. We did an underground survey and I took the drawings with me. Mies looked at them and said: "Oh my God, I cannot do this. It is impossible."

The underground survey showed the subway, the Bank station, a post office, endless public utilities. "How can I navigate my way, into putting foundations for a building? Is there a part of this site which is free of underground encumbrances?" And there was, on the extreme West side of the site; there was this patch of land. Mies said: "This is where the building has to go."

Because he wanted to build only on 22% of the entire site, what happened was that the building was placed there and it released at its base an area of about 100 by 80 yards, quite big, which became a square. That was the setting, not only for the building, but also to reveal the chronology of distinguished buildings that surrounded it, including the Mansion House by George Dance, not to mention incorporating the ceremonials associated with the City of London, which have never been given the importance that, perhaps, they deserve.

So it was purely practical considerations that prompted the siting of Mies building - and he saw it at once, he saw it in few minutes.

Anyway thank you for your commitment and energy: without you, Peter, no Poultry. Did the process turn out to be very difficult?

It was enormously difficult. The City wanted to be sure that if planning permission was granted, the development would go ahead, it did not want any loose ends to frustrate the development. And so what they said in the late 1960s early 1970s was: "We will give you provisional planning permission; and when you have secured the site and bought the outstanding interests, we would give you full planning permission."

Well, it took 13 years to acquire the site, to translate the 40% into 100%. And when we went back, in the 1980s, they said: "We are sorry. Policy has changed. Preservation is the principal objective now and you want to tear down Victorian buildings." They listed part of the lot and made a new conservation area - it was outside the conservation area at the time. They did everything they could to frustrate development.

Now the Victorian buildings were, with one exception, of very little consequences. I had enlisted the support of John Summerson, who was director of the Soane Museum and the recognised authority on Georgian and Victorian architecture. A wonderful man. He came out in favour of Mies's (and Jim's) schemes, writing a very good letter to *The Times*, to start with. He was one of those men, I have met one or two of them in my life, who when you ask them a question they sort of look up to the ceiling, and they do not say anything, and time goes by, and you think, "Oh, God! Did he hear my question?" And suddenly, perhaps a couple of minutes later, they start talking. He was one of those. Actually Mies was another one, he needed to be lubricated, to really become expansive and to trust you.

Of course the conservationists and the preservationists were outraged that Sir John Summerson should come out in favour of Mies. Summerson thought that Mies was a great architect. He placed very little value in the Victorian buildings on site, rightly. Because it was a superfluous piece of land created by driving through Queen Victoria Street, in the early 1870s, into Bank junction and it just left this triangular site. These buildings had no proper foundations, none of them aligned with one another, it was a jumble of sort of Venetian/Gothic late Victorian buildings. There was only one building of merit, at the corner, which was by the architect John Belcher.

The planning committee was opposed to anything that we put forward, they continuously turned us down, and were totally hostile. We had, against us, SAVE, English Heritage, we had the police, taxi drivers and everybody. On our side we had John Summerson, Richard Rogers, Norman Foster, Berthold Lubetkin and Jim Stirling. We persevered, and this eventually led to the first Public Inquiry. It was difficult, it really was, but it was worth it.

You managed to upset Prince Charles. He is opinionated about architecture and he does not like me. It can happen. What was your main argument with him?

His main argument was expressed, out of the blue, on a beautiful evening in June at Hampton Court, outside the City. It was the occasion upon which the Prince of Wales was going to give the Royal Gold Medal for Architecture to Charles Correa, in 1984. There were 600 people there - I was one of them - and it was followed by a dinner.

Suddenly the Prince produced his own speech, that he had written himself - he did not read the speech that had been prepared for him. It was a diatribe against modern architecture. It was against the work of Richard, Norman, ABK's National Gallery proposal in Trafalgar Square. There were shots aimed at Mansion House Square: you have to remember that this was just at the time of the Public Inquiry.

Charles Correa, the recipient, and Norman Foster, who was also there, came over quite slowly, put their arms around my shoulders and said: "Do not worry. You know it is going to be alright." Well, of course it was not alright, because two days later we were in Court

- we resumed the Public Inquiry - and the Queen's Counsel, who was opposed to us, got up and said to the Inspector: "We have a very important witness we would like to call to express his views, but he is not readily available though we would like to bring him along."

Now that was pure theatre, they were talking about the Prince of Wales. I think he was the one who was responsible, really, for the defeat of Mies's project.

The Ministry report said that Mies's building was bad, bad manners, it did not respect the context in which it was being placed and it infringed the view of St Paul's Cathedral from hole 17 of the Sydenham Hill Golf Club, miles away. And it was rejected.

The door was left open, slightly. There was a caveat, indeed, with words to the effect that if the developer could put forward an alternative design that was respectful - that was good mannered, well mannered - and that was in keeping with the grain and the rhythm of the city of London, the project could be reconsidered.

I made it my business to go around the City of London to the great and the good: to the Governor of the Bank of England, to the chairman of the Stock Exchange and to people in positions of power. "I am here as a humble developer, and this is the situation: I have just been turned down for a building designed by Mies van der Rohe. What would you do in my place, as an alternative? Who would you go to?" And of course nobody had an idea. Nothing. But, at the same time, they all said the same thing: whatever you do, build within the grain and the context of the city.

That is why we went straight to Jim, who was very well disposed towards Mies, because he had been kind to him. Indeed, when Jim first went to Chicago and knew nobody in the city, Mies invited him to dinner. And Jim never forgot it. So he had given evidence, very good evidence, for Mies and made very interesting remarks about his design.

I had met Jim for the first in the United States then, later, he came to France and stayed with us. Also, I have this personal memory of Jim, who was very interested when I bought the Maisons Jaoul, and said that they had an influence on Chandigarh. We both enjoyed wine - and the drinking of it.

I am almost 20 years old, I am grown up, but I cannot see many young buildings with the same character today. Do you agree?

Yes, I agree, I cannot see many buildings with the same character today. When Jim designed you, Poultry, he designed you as a partner among equals - there was no hostility toward other buildings or distinctions surrounding your site.

There are two ledges at the top of your rostral column, that people had been calling two ears: Jim would not like this, because the ledges were connections between his building and the church by Wren, St Stephen Walbrook (to the South-East) and Lutyens's building (on the North side). They were just having a respectful dialogue as friends. There was no attempt to compete, it was a wonderful way of demonstrating a sort of democratic decision, a conversation between inanimate objects that, nevertheless, speak volumes.

And I do not see any patrons like you around, only people concerned with the bottom line in London.

I think that the problem with patronage - or a lack of it - is that development is carried out by developers who have no concern for their artistic legacy. Developers are beholden to shareholders or people whose principal concern is that they want to see a quick return on their money; and if there is any delay in the planning process, or in anything else, then they apply pressure on the developer. When you plant a tree I always take the view that you plant it for your grandchildren, you cannot hurry the growth of the tree, it has to evolve. And if you try to hurry, it probably dies. Now it is not an exact analogy, but there is organic growth in both.

The downside of patronage is that you get patrons, I think, who tell the architect what to do. I have always tried to avoid that, because I do not think you go to Picasso and ask him to paint your portrait and then tell him how to paint, and what you want to see, and try to control the whole thing; otherwise why go to Picasso? Personally speaking, I think you have to give the minimum information, which I did to Jim and to Mies, and let them generate a creative process, in their own way, in their own time.

[with] Michael Wilford

Can you tell me something about Jim?

Our relationship was, in some ways, complicated and schizophrenic. The atmosphere in the office was quite strict and totally focused on the work - although always accompanied by music on BBC Radio 3. There were occasional jokes, but it was very intense. In contrast, outside the office and whenever we travelled together, Jim exposed a completely different aspect of his personality. He was more relaxed, more open and more friendly, but as soon as we returned to the office everything became proper and correct again.

Our professional relationship developed and changed over 32 years from the time I began working with him in a Master/Assistant relationship, to the later years of our partnership when we worked together on an equal basis.

He was a secretive person, keeping his private life very separate from the office. I remember an extraordinary train journey we made together in the mid 1960s to Middlesbrough when we were involved with the Dorman Long Headquarters project. He suddenly exclaimed: "I got married yesterday." We knew nothing of his plans and the office was very surprised at the news. Apparently it was, characteristically, a short, sharp ceremony with just three close friends present.

His behaviour towards people who he felt were not in tune with him was abrupt and he did not suffer fools gladly. I remember on one occasion whilst developing the details of the Leicester University Engineering building we needed some technical advice on the proposed elevators. A gentleman arrived at the office, formally dressed, wearing a bowler hat, carrying a rolled umbrella and leather briefcase. We started to ask questions and it soon became clear that he was a salesman and knew nothing about the technicalities of elevators. Jim quickly became irritated and told him to leave the office immediately!

He was often intolerant of planners, particularly those with dogmatic, negative attitudes who, rather than conducting a constructive dialogue to find the best solution for the building and its context, had only one word in their vocabulary: No!

On the contrary, his working relationship with Peter Rees, the City of London Planning Officer, was very positive. It was interesting to witness him, unaccustomed to tolerating people who were not tuned into the same frequency, exercising the diplomacy necessary to gain acceptance of the design of a building.

The striking thing about his attitude to design was his sheer tenacity: despite all complications and setbacks Jim rarely became disheartened or annoyed - or did not express it. Looking back, his perseverance and design ingenuity in responding to problems and constructive criticism by enhancing the project rather than undermining it, was amazing.

You were travelling around when I was young, you and Jim had these American dreams - did you neglect me?

No. Not at all. My involvement with you was limited at certain stages because I was looking after the two projects we had in progress in America at that time. This involved a lot of travelling and time being spent away from the office in London.

Jim's attention was fully focused on your conception. Later I became involved in the development of your design and its difficult birth, particularly the mass of documentation necessary for the Public Inquiry to which the design was subjected prior to receiving planning permission. We could not both travel to America and leave you languishing unattended!

There were two alternative projects for the site:
what would my sister have been like?

There is no doubt that if the Mappin & Webb building had been retained, your sister would not have been as beautiful as you. We conceived your sister in order to demonstrate your strengths as the best design. You were both presented to the authorities as equals but privately I thought that, if built, your sister would have been rather fat and ugly.

They all call me Postmodern. What do people mean when they call me that?

I do not know what Postmodern means either, particularly when applied to architecture. So I do not understand that description of you. You have a privileged position amongst an amazing collection of buildings at the centre of the City of London. Your form and dress were conceived as signals of a meaningful future for urban architecture - looking forward as well as back. You are not "Post" anything.

I believe Postmodern is an inaccurate and irrelevant description. You were designed as a contrast to the Mies van der Rohe project, which was a singular tower building relying for its character on a singular form, choice of material and refinement of detail. You are a formal composition of a variety of geometric elements organised and articulated both horizontally and vertically around a central axis. You are a clear composition of contrasting pieces, somewhat reminiscent of the earlier buildings on the site. At the same time you represent yourself as one building with wit and playfulness in your massing and façades which is very much of its time but based on the principles of clear, classical composition.

You respect your neighbours and the history of architecture. You also carry forward the activities in and around your skirts. You contain architectural ideas that were not only relevant to the time in which you were conceived, but which I believe are applicable to the situation today.

25

You once whispered to me that at the time there were five architectural critics in the newspapers. Did I and my peers have an impact on society that is now lost?

Yes! Unfortunately the design of cities and buildings appears to be of diminishing interest and concern of the general public, commerce and politicians to the detriment of our culture and wellbeing. You were fortunate to be the prodigy of an enlightened, passionate and committed patron of the arts.

Architectural media coverage and criticism is in a bad way. Few national newspapers now have regular architectural coverage compared with several years ago when most serious publications could justify the expense and effort of having a correspondent visit buildings and write about them. So much of current so called criticism is merely a recycling of PR press releases issued by clients and architects. There is little objective, independent coverage of architecture in current media.

[with] Laurence Bain

How do you remember my conception and birth?

Ours was not an office where Jim sketched a concept and passed it along to the other people working on the project. When we started working on you at an early project stage there were three of us in the front room of Gloucester Place and Jim was in the back room with Michael; and what he would ask us to do was to come up with a project that met the requirements of the brief, that took account of all the surroundings of the site and respected the rules, as perhaps defined by the City Plan.

Within a broad framework, we were charged as individuals and as a group, to come up with as many ideas, as many solutions as possible to that problem. So we would, for five-six days, just brainstorm ideas for the site: and each of these ideas we would give a name to, so we would call them "the dart scheme", "the symmetry scheme", so that your possible forms would be memorable for Jim. This was important because at some time, maybe weeks later, maybe months later, Jim would say: "Did we do something in 'the dart scheme' that we can take into this scheme?" So in this first instance we would come up immediately with some twenty different alternatives, and we would sit around the table and describe the concepts we had proposed. At the start of the design process Jim always wanted to have orthographic drawings, plans and sections and massing drawings; he did not want any detail, or fenestration, just the outlines firstly at a scale of 1:1250 and then as we moved on 1:500. It would then be edited, so he would say: "Well, I quite like 'the dart scheme' and I quite like that piece from that scheme, go and see if you can come up with something else within those parameters." We would then go back into the front room and spend the next week drawing up various options. Jim was then editing the whole thing in his head, and you could see him thinking about it. And he would never reject anything, it was only a matter of which was the better direction to go in. And slowly, over this period of time, you, the building would be conceived: at first as a concept, an idea and that idea became, in a sense, the reason for you to be born as an entity that can be drawn in much more detail and with much more accuracy.

I remember also how important the use of the models was to overcome some difficult situations. We were fundamentally a drawing office and Jim would usually design buildings by means of drawings - very precise, very accurate drawings. But in this instance, since we had some historical material from Mies, and Jim particularly liked a 1:1250 model, he used the model as a way of developing the design process. He would also use it when we had to do presentations to various bodies within the greater community, something he did not like. We would take along the models and he would use them to describe your design to individuals. Jim usually concluded the presentation by lifting out the little triangular model that would fit in the palm of your hand and passing it over to the person he was presenting at to, like a petit four - "Look, look how lovely this is, would you like to hold this object, this piece of jewellery, it is going to be magnificent when we get it built..."

Do you remember how Jim defended me during the Public Inquiry?

Jim did not like the Public Inquiry process. I think Jim believed that as an esteemed architect he should automatically have sufficient status and that going into the analysis of the "right and wrongs" of a project should be totally unnecessary. But we knew from the start that there was a high possibility that we would have to go through the Public Inquiry process. And this involved writing a proof of evidence that Jim would give at the Public Inquiry to the inspectors. This process follows the procedural rules, and has to cover things that have not only to do with architectural design, but with justifying the mix of commercial spaces, defending the proposal in terms of planning law; it is a multi-layered process I basically wrote Jim's proof of evidence for the inquiry, the first draft, and then Jim went through it and meticulously edited it and corrected it - he did not like the "flowery language"; and I have all of these documents, with Jim changing words and phrases within the structure of the evidence of the Public Inquiry. At the Public Inquiry itself I sat alongside Jim when he was giving evidence – he had to ask for special permission, it was unusual. Of course Jim, being very graphical, wanted to rely on all the drawings that had been produced; and we produced some beautiful and very precise drawings for the inquiry. Jim went through the text and pointed out various aspects of your design on the drawings to explain them. Then, at the end of this process, both our side and the other side could ask Jim questions, and he did not like this - too many technical questions in legal language. He did not like being asked the sort of questions that had nothing to do with the architecture and his design philosophy. But there was one question that he did particularly like. The Inspector said: "What about presence? Does your building have presence?" And Jim then spent half an hour discussing your presence in architectural terms and whether, for example, a chair in a room would have presence. And this philosophical discussion was really interesting - all the lawyers were just falling asleep, but Jim was very much engaged with the Inspector, which basically goes back to the point I mentioned earlier: that Jim was interested in this sort of "architecture of life", but he was not interested in anything else.

What aspects of the design did you imagine would be controversial?

People in the office believed in Jim. So if Jim pushed a particular direction, he did not often bother to explain things. For example, if you take the tower at your corner, One Poultry, the way it is articulated: we did that, we drew various options - and Jim would suggest a direction and we believed it, we thought "This is the right way to do it." It was only subsequently that people like Sandy Wilson said "This is a rostral column with maritime allusions," or someone else said "This has to do with some of the visions of Léon Krier." Well, Jim would never say "This is a rostral column"; we were not designing things for the sake of comment, analysis or surprise.

It was difficult to get me built. Do you remember some of the crucial episodes?

There was also "the other side" as we called them, those groups who wanted to save the previous heritage, which is part of a democratic process - we live in a democracy. In planning terms, indeed, you were seen as a battle between contemporary architecture and historic architecture. It is this battle that people usually see as critical to your birth. For me, instead, the time when you may not have made it was in 1993. When a project is to be built in a conservation area, you have to let the construction contract for the development of the whole project before you can demolish the building on the site. Once we had planning permission from the Secretary of State, we had five years to start construction before the permission would run out. We had legal challenges and then to obtain a road closure of Bucklersbury - this took time, years - and then we had to find a contractor, who was willing to sign the agreement for the construction of the whole building, which was required to be built in a very limited five-year period. The lawyers had to write a contract and we had to produce drawings and specifications. We had a signed construction contract one week before the deadline ran out: it was an absolute critical period in terms of your birth as a building. If we had not managed to do that, we could have not built you. This is the story of the challenges of your birth as a building that often gets forgotten: many unnamed people believed that you'd turn out well.

And were there any pleasant surprises?

Two or three years ago I was on your roofgarden and there was a tall person standing, looking down through the geometries, watching the people scurrying back and forward across from work and going to Cannon Street Station. The place was really buzzing and he turned around at me and said: "Do you know this building?" And I said "Yes, I was involved a little bit."
"This is such a cool building." I immediately thought "cool" would never be a word of Jim's vocabulary; but the fact that you were so alive in the 21st century, was a pleasant surprise...

[with] Peter Rees

Can you tell me something about Mies's project?

I can tell you very little about Mies's project, because I arrived to take up my post in charge of planning the City of London in 1985, when it had already been rejected and the Public Inquiry over the appeal had been lost. I had only been following the Mies project at a distance, from another post elsewhere in London.

However, when the press contacted me, just before I took up my new post, they wanted my opinion on what should happen, as the Mies project was not acceptable. To me, the fundamental problem with the Mies project related its townscape and urban design. It had a poor relationship with the surrounding buildings and the pattern of the place. For over a hundred years the City had met at a point with roads radiating from the Bank Junction - largely a Victorian creation, when roads like Queen Victoria Street and King William Street were cut through the city fabric, nevertheless, this was the focus of the city. The overall concept of the Mies scheme was that to accommodate a rectangular building, which Mies's buildings were by and large, it was necessary to refashion the form of the city to fit his design.

Mies proposed a new Mansion House Square, but this was a square which leaked in all directions and exposed buildings elevations which were never meant to be seen. It exposed the side elevation of the Mansion House, it exposed an uncomfortable view of St Stephen's Walbrook Church and removed an adjacent triangular Victorian building, built for the National Safe Deposit Company (now the City of London Magistrate's Court). Worst of all it opened up a "full-frontal" view of the Lutyens's 27 Poultry, former headquarters of the Midland Bank. Now anyone who had studied that elevation would realise that Lutyens designed the building never to be seen front on. In elevation it appears to be very crudely detailed building, because it was designed to be appreciated from a very acute angle, either along Cheapside or from Lombard Street and in both of those views it is absolutely magnificent. When the Number One Poultry site was cleared, it was possible to see the front of the Lutyens building from a distance for the first time and its exaggerated details looked grotesque, because the architect had never intended it to be seen in this way.

The Mies scheme would have created a square with a road through and opened views of buildings never meant to be seen, either than in passing. All this to make the right shaped site for Mies's concept. As an architect/planner this is not the way I work: I like buildings to actually be sensitive to their location. They should have a rational relationship with their surroundings and fit their site - otherwise, it is like having the wrong piece in the jigsaw.

Did you like me from the beginning?

Your birth was a difficult one. You did not look the way you look now, when you were first conceived. In fact, you were conceived as twins, as two potential projects: one of which was a tall building, leaving a triangular space in front of it, not unlike the mistake that the Mies building would have made; and another, which was a triangular block filling the site. It was only one of these which I supported, the one that fitted the location.

I liked the triangular you, I did not like the tall you with space in front. However, even the triangular you, once it had become the preferred conception, had a difficult gestation and birth, because there were many people involved, not all of whom approved of you being born at all. I was one of the few outside the development team who supported and approved of you from your conception, even if I did see that there were some shortcomings that needed to be addressed before you were ready to face the world.

I find it really strange to be speaking to a building!

Those other chaps in the City Planning Office, what were their concerns?

You were born into a city with a long history and you were to take up your place, on a site which also had a considerable back story. This was a site occupied by buildings that had grown in an organic sort of way to fill their site, full of a mixture of uses, that had been there for some time and which were loved by many people. They had architectural character, especially the Mappin & Webb building at the Bank junction, occupying a site with remnants of a medieval street pattern. Many people did not want to see you born, because you were going to disrupt their beloved and familiar territory. Also the original buildings were occupied by many small businesses who would not survive the process of being displaced: they were very strongly opposed to your birth and also had a strong political influence on the City Corporation through its elected members. All these forces were pressing very strongly for an abortion.

I understand that all my stripes can seem out of place.
What did you think about them?

It was understood from the beginning that the design you would present to the outside world, your façades, would reflect the age in which you were designed, rather than hiding under camouflage or being a pastiche of the buildings on adjoining sites. It was not a matter of how much I liked your outer appeareance: for me the important things were the uses which you would contain and the way that your mass and form related to the surroundings and to the site on which you were to live. Therefore, to me the stripes were never a strong issue, they were part of your character, part of your parentage, but not necessarily a planning issue - I felt they were more a matter of taste than planning practice. Personally, I am pleased that you have two kinds of skin: one kind of skin from Gloucestershire and the other from New South Wales. I am always pleased to see and touch the warm biscuit sandstone of Sidney and to rub against the beautiful pink/red sandstone of a favourite English county. Bringing these two visually-contrasted materials, with great physical similarity together, in a place that is a world centre, seems most appropriate. The Bank junction has often been called "the heart of the Empire" - I correct that by saying it should be "the wallet of the Empire"; nevertheless, it is certainly the centre of an international web of business contacts, well represented by your diverse skin.

Today, would you support another building like me?

I dislike similar buildings in the same place, unless in a homogenous city townscape like Bath. I like heterogeneity; buildings that contrast with one another in their designs, so that we understand each building independently from the others. At the same time, buildings should say polite things to one another through their materials, scale and form and I believe you do that.

On any other site, the architectural solution would be a different one. To have two of you would not be appropriate, unless there happened to be absolutely identical circumstances, which is very unlikely.

What is this fifth elevation?

At a relatively late stage in your design, I saw models and drawings which showed a fifth elevation or "roof-scape", that was purely flat. You looked very much like a post-modern "aircraft carrier", with a feature-less flat roof. I explained to the people who were representing you that the design needed a silhouette, if I was to have any chance of gaining planning permission for you. Although I supported the scheme - your massing, bulk, and general design - the lack of a skyline was a weakness which would make it hard to convince those who needed to grant permission that you should be allowed to exist.

Now, your conception was a difficult one; your architect, Jim Stirling, would not talk to planners - he did not like planners - and only the project architect, Laurence Bain, would come to visit me; your client, Lord Palumbo, Peter Palumbo as he then was, would not see me, as he was hurt by his experience in losing the Mies van der Rohe scheme, of which he was so fond.

And therefore I was in a difficult situation, unable to talk to the key players in your design. I managed to convince Simon Harris, the property representative, that I needed to speak to Jim directly, if I was going to be able to influence your design in a way that would be likely to gain planning permission.

A meeting was arranged with Peter Palumbo, where I was vetted for my support for the scheme. A few days later my PA announced: "I have Jim's Stirling's secretary on the phone, he says you're to be in his office at 11 o'clock this morning." This was not the normal way of doing things. But I was up for a challenge, so I set off for Fitzroy Square; I was greeted and shown up to the studio, where Jim turned off the classical music on Radio 3, sat down with me and said: "What do you want?"
I answered: "I am trying to support your scheme and I feel that without a skyline and an active fifth elevation, it will be difficult to gain permission."
And Jim: "What do you mean, what do you want on the roof?"
I answered: "Well, this is not really my job, you are the architect, but maybe a garden, or perhaps a restaurant, something that would animate the roof, and also create an interesting skyline."
He said: "I see, I understand, you can go now."

About two weeks later the same procedure, "Mr Stirling wishes to see you in his office at 11 o'clock" and I proceeded once more to Fitzroy Square; again, the music was turned down and a model was produced - a flat model, simply of a roof garden and a restaurant - the rest of the building was absent. Jim said to me: "Is that what you want?"
I answered: "It looks very interesting, but how does it look on top of the building?"

"That's nothing to do with you, I am the architect. You can go now."

And so I retreated, having at least influenced the use and appereance of your roof. Even with this change I failed by one vote to gain
support for you at the planning committee, in spite of my impas-
sioned presentation, which lasted three quarters of an hour.

Nevertheless, eventually, you were conceived following appeals at
every judicial level in the Land up to the House of Lords, which was
then our Supreme Court - I am so pleased that in those days there
was no European Court, otherwise things might have gone the
other way.

[with] Charles Jencks

I understand there are unpublished interviews you did with Jim,
where he reveals the British animus against his work.

I talked to Jim a lot about his frustrations, the attacks on him, when he was trying to build for the British and how his first jobs were turned down by the denizens of suburbia as "aesthetically sub-standard". For someone who set out to be the number one British architect - and became so, with his late modern and postmodern landmarks of Leicester and Stuttgart - it was a galling insult. He well understood what aesthetics were, particularly the aesthetics of architecture. And because of these early experiences, he later said, "architects in Britain should talk only of function to their client, not aesthetics - or else they'll lose the job."

Aside from the attacks on me, what were the main ones?

He provoked conflict with his university buildings at St Andrews, Cambridge and Oxford, and when he designed the building in Haslemere, for Olivetti. There he went through 17 colour changes, because of the local taste: 16 of them were refused! Or so he told me with bitter humour. He invited me to the opening, and showed me the colours he wanted. Contrasting ones, a kind of a lemon-green versus vibrant purple, like Michael Wilford's purple shirts - you can find them on the interior radiators. Jim said his original combination was like a Edwardian Marquee next to the existing Edwardian country house - a surprisingly vital contextualism (as he saw it). The aesthetic arbitrators said: "No, you cannot have these two garish colours, you must change." And finally he was forced into the contrast between mushroom and blancmange - the two most unobtrusive colours possible. They concluded: "If we followed your colours, they would have frightened away the birds." So Jim was beaten up by British provinciality, conventional taste and small mindedness.

They "killed" him at least twice: at the beginning of his career in 1963 with Leicester, and then with another one of his late modern buildings, the Runcorn housing. For this scheme I witnessed Prince Charles attacking him at the grand Mansion House dinner of 1987, in front of the architectural and City establishment, a humiliating and insensitive thing to do if, like the Prince, you are trying to win over architects to your "Vision for Britain". One of the unpublished things Jim said to me, was: "If I win the competition for the Disney Concert House in Los Angeles (which Frank Gehry ultimately won), I will emigrate."

So what was the ultimate upshot of these attacks and defeats?

But getting the commission for you, Poultry, *Numero Uno* in the City, and in the midst of all that architecture - near St Mary Woolnoth by his great predecessor Hawksmoor (whom he loved) - was his revenge. Served up cold in eternal stone right opposite the Mansion House. When novelists come to write about this, the ironies will be worthy of Jonathan Swift or Evelyn Waugh. For Prince Charles again attacked the new Stirling scheme, for looking like a "1930s wireless"; but he lost his *Battle of the Radio* at the Public Inquiry. The scheme is a text-book example of Post-Modern contextualism; but may look like an Art Deco Wireless from a Royal helicopter.

Did he work hard to design me?

Stirling slaved endlessly, especially on the *compositional* ideas: one experiment after another, intending to make it a supreme perform-ance, a lesson to the British, or *Stirling 'Dimostrazioni'* as Alvin Bo-yarsky called his didactic architecture aimed at showing the British how to do the right thing. After all, your site is called "Number One Poultry", the Ground Zero of Britain. Jim is effectively saying: "after 30-40 years of humiliation I am getting even, by producing a superb 'pyjama building', in my late Post-Modern, Striped Style." Of course, he liked none of these stylistic labels, which all did apply, and did enjoy sending up his critics - even sympathetic ones like me.

38

It is extraordinary how some English critics hated him, and this building, like Gavin Stamp. I remember walking down the corridor of power with Jim and Richard Rogers, at their Royal Academy exhibit in 1986, when Gavin approached. Jim and Richard, traumatised by his reviews, gave him a wide berth and the "evil-eye".

So such reactions provoked low intensity warfare?

British taste, which can be violently censorious, either directly or indirectly, had taken its toll on Jim. Your appereance provokes debate: "Look, I am going to show you how it is done; how you make bold contrasting architecture great again, in the Hawksmoor manner." You make a strong, visual, geometrical, complex statement about the past, the present and the future. Thus you are a classic postmodern building, the best in this country, full stop. Better than Venturi's National Gallery; Jim was very upset not to win that competition, especially to lose it to the American postmodernist.

But then, am I really postmodern? I don't understand this word.

Quite right, no one understands the word, it is an open word, it has many meanings. You could say, to simplify, that all postmodernists are pluralists, radical pluralists - the pluralism is political as well as market-oriented. But market pluralism is not "true" pluralism and Postmodernism is about "true" pluralism. Because it is always about the other, about difference, about complexity in a plural global culture, which is searching what architecture should be about, in the age of iconic building.

In 2001, Venturi famously said (paraphrasing the McCarthy era): "I have never been and I am not now, a member of the postmodern party." And Jim said more or less the same thing to me (which I quoted on the back of *Post-Modern Classicism*, 1985). Like Groucho Marx, Jim and Venturi "would never join a club that would have him." They were both disturbed by their followers - that is why they did not like the label.

I was very close to Jim, for many years. His reluctance to admit Postmodernism, has dissuaded a lot of critics from using that PoMo word. Jim used to say to me: "I like everything you write about my work, except the word Postmodernism."
"Why, Jim?"
"I just do not like the people who are postmodern in this country, I think they are terrible architects."
"That is no reason to object to a term."
And then Jim said: "Well, I have always been the same, anyway. What I have done is always the same."
"Come on Jim, you are an architect, but I am an historian and critic, it is my job to tell you if you are doing the same, not your job to tell it!"

He denied that he was a postmodernist. It tells you something important, it tells you that there is a dark side, in the post-fact era of Trump, that there is a great downside to Postmodernism.

I attacked the misuse of the label a lot myself, and I can see that when Stirling proclaims his allegiance to the modernist tradition, in a sense he is going back to something that he has in his imagination about Modernism, which is important to him.

There is no question he has a paternity suit for Postmodernism, he is father of the movement, like Venturi. And you cannot undo history.

1978, *Roma Interrotta* exhibition. That is a big moment for Postmodernism, which usually does not get the right attention. By then Jim is part of a world movement, of "stage one". Then it occurs, as always, that the style is commercialised within ten years and it is a catastrophe. In the arts and architecture, every movement since 1800 has been corrupted, however successful it is.

Ruskin once said: "I cannot stand Ruskinian Gothic." Many significant leaders like Nietzsche, Marx and Freud denied their influences, especially over wayward followers (as they saw them) and said they were not a "Nietzschean", "Marxist" or "Freudian"...

Denying influence is an all too human frailty. This is also true of architects, as part of movements, who refuse to admit their influence, because it is watered-down and vulgarised: while it should be accepted with a certain amount of grace.

I feel a bit like a hipster in a suit. It seemed necessary with these neighbours.

In London there are one or two places where the British establishment displays itself, such as Buckingham Palace or in a club, where you have to wear a suit and tie. You have to make stylistic concessions, especially if you are a rebel.

Of course by the time Jim came along, Pop Art was happening, and he was on the edge of the movement. And he also realised that royalty, for instance Princess Diana, could be a hipster on occasion. It had become completely conventional to wear a bespoke suit set off by a garishly prole tie. This postmodern double-coding was common since the 1960s, since Robert Rauschenberg's art and the Independent Group of 1956 started it all (which Jim used to attend). Nothing new there!

Can you explain these oppositions, the ones that I embody?

Perhaps some. As usual, there is a little bit of Constructivism in the "diving boards" at the end, on either side of the central, cylindrical tower, which marks the place, Number One, and turns the corner. Now everybody wonders: "Why do you have two diving boards that cantilever off the sides, like ears of a face?" Visually they are very necessary, and Jim inserted them in with a great, heroic sense, as he did with many motifs.

There are obvious, classical references, which people have picked up, like squaring the circle, really triangulating the circle if you look at the plan. Thus you find variations on all the classical and Platonic forms throughout the building. Jim was a part-classicist since 1972, he told me, when the classical exhibition came to the Tate. He was trained by Colin Rowe, and that means Italian classicism, as well as the volumetric kind Jim learned from Le Corbusier.

Then there are all the urban references, of which he, I think, was a design-pioneer: the Dusseldorf scheme, an incredible piece of Postmodernism, in 1975, which led immediately to Stuttgart, 1977, which became *the* kind of hard-core postmodern contextualism. You do fit into the context *but* you bring it alive, by making variations and critiques of it. His design for you, Poultry, picks up what I have described as the mid-scale façade (between the smaller classical scale and the huge modern box). Jim then modulates this solution with an "angular" curve; and then syncopates the combined motif at an angle. That syncopation is very much in Jim's, but it stems from Le Corbusier's language of architectural form.

In a way, I think that your quotes, are also from within his own corpus, quoting himself and his pyjama game, for example. I cannot remember where this starts, but it is basically the old rustication of "ABAB stripes" as you go up the façade, with different courses, which he does in so many 1970s buildings. Stuttgart is importantly a more subtle "ABAB" rhythm; it is done well in Stuttgart and in your case, Poultry; but sometimes too stridently in America. I was reading that someone said that there are two shades of pink at Poultry: I do not know if that is true, I haven't seen them, but that is what critics who do *not* like it may see.

There are many more references you could pick up: there is a Bernini *Scala Regia*, which is in search of the Royalty. Then there is the architectural promenade, which is a Le Corbusier idea of a heroic passage through the building, from the beginning to the culmination: Michael Wilford does it very well, in his British Embassy in Berlin. You can say in a walkthrough of your building, you walk up the *Scala Regia* and then you experience the public realm in the curve, then you go up to the top, and as in Le Corbusier's buildings you have a cosmic unfolding of the universe right out into the garden, and then the horizon. What could be better as a promenade?

*With the demolition of Pruitt Igoe, you say Postmodernism starts in
architecture [1972]; does it finish with my completion [1998]?*

You could say it does finish with your completion, with the first
stage of Postmodernism – "complexity one". That period really starts
on a wonderful scale with Venturi's thoughts of 1965, and Jim's
buildings. Stuttgart is, for me, the greatest early building of Postmodernism and in Britain that stage culminates in Poultry.

There is a straight line from Stuttgart to Poultry. The metaphor, the
feeling for the body and the face, the mixture of the past and the
future. Above all, the acknowledging of time is extremely important
in Jim's work and he understands all that, just as Umberto Eco understands the question of time in his book *The Name of the Rose*
- and Eco uses architecture to explain it.

That is only the first stage of Postmodernism, and its first demise.
Poultry, you happened to be born at a wrong time, the nadir of the
older postmodern fashion. But in 1997, one year before you were
completed, it was "reborn again" with Frank Gehry at Bilbao.
In the 15th century architects reused the rebirth metaphor many
times. Postmodernism II, "complexity two" was now computerised,
ornament was digitised and PoMo roared back by 2000, in all ways
except in name. At it helm was the latest tradition of iconic buildings, those that communicate strongly through metaphors: good
buildings and questionable ones.

"Poultry" talks to the City, in a way that it is better than the "Shard,"
which talks a little bit to the boats and steeples; or the "Gherkin",
another postmodern iconic building, which also talks to a lot of important things like the pineapple & pinecone and Fibonacci Series,
and ecology. But we also get too many one-liner icons: epitomised
by the "Walkie-Talkie". Or the "Cheesegrater" - which is, however,
a structurally interesting building.

Poultry, in urbanistic terms, you are still an unbeaten chicken.

43

Poultry, you are a very meaningful act in four or five ways; although not always explicitly. What, however, is very explicit is your vitality and expression, your colour and strength of form. In these ways, Jim did much better than Lutyens next door, and the other classical architects who failed to rise to the occasion. Poultry, you are like Hawksmoor's building, vitally alive in a way that blows away Baker's Bank of England - a contextual building, which makes the others look rigid and embarrassed. You enjoy yourself, a mood that got up the nose of some critics because you had the guts to broadcast architectural pleasure. That meaning is palpable. Go inside the open public triangle and see those dark blue, shiny bricks, so unexpected in a classical context of circling the triangle that it makes you laugh - with a little gasp. Such are the wake-up details. Jim wants to provoke, he's another *agent provocateur* in the long history of Modernism, Postmodernism, the Parthenon and Pantheon, all wake-up calls of architecture waiting for the public to answer the phone.

Further Readings

Hugh Pearman, 'PoMo's back in fashion', *RIBA Journal*, vol. 124, no. 1 (2017), p. 59.

Catherine Croft, 'London Po-Mo', *C20*, no. 2 (2016), p. 32-38.

Richard Waite, 'Twentieth Century Society makes listing bid for No. 1 Poultry', *Architects' Journal*, vol. 241, no. 23 (2015), p. 5.

'Stirling revisited: Buckley Grey Yeoman eyes on No.1 Poultry revamp', *Architects' Journal*, vol. 240, no. 13 (2014), p. 7.

Mike Booth and others, 'Number 1, Poultry, City of London', *Arup Journal*, vol. 34, no. 2 (1999), p. 3-8.

Colin St John Wilson, 'City Prize: Stirling at Poultry', *Architecture Today*, no. 91 (1998), p. 52-73.

Kenneth Powell, Robert Maxwell, 'Stirling's City legacy', *Architect's Journal*, vol. 208, no. 17 (1998), p. 33-43.

David Watkin, Piers Gough, 'Were the conservationists right?', *RIBA Journal*, vol. 104, no. 10 (1997), p. 30-31.

Gus Alexander, 'Chicken coup [No. 1 Poultry, City of London]', *Building*, vol. 262, no. 8010/40 (1997), p. 40-41.

'Palumbo switches on his wireless set', *Building*, vol. 258, no. 7811/38 (1993), p. 10.

Colin St John Wilson and others, 'Poultry n.1 in London', *Zodiac*, no. 3 (1990), p. 62-97.

Peter Buchanan, 'La clave del contexto: James Stirling en Londres', *Arquitectura Viva*, no. 5 (1989), p. 14-16.

Paul Finch, Gavin Stamp, 'Symbolic city victory for Stirling and Palumbo', *Building Design*, no. 941 (1989), p. 2-3.

'Stirling's big bang in London', *Architectural Record*, vol. 176, no. 4 (1988), p. 55.

Peter Buchanan, 'Stirling in context', *Architect's Journal*, vol. 187, no. 18 (1988), p. 24-29.

'Jekyll and Hyde: two tales of the City', *Blueprint*, no. 39 (1987), p. 4.

'English Heritage supports Palumbo', *Building*, vol. 251, no. 7461/36 (1986), p. 9.

Daralice Donkervoet Boles, 'Palumbo's encore: Stirling stars', *Progressive Architecture*, vol. 67, no. 7 (1986), p. 23, 39.

James Stirling, Michael Wilford & Associates, 'No 1 Poultry, London EC4', *Architectural Design*, vol. 56, no. 5 (1986), p. 28-39.

Thomas Muirhead, Colin Rowe and Robert Kahn, 'Stirling since Stuttgart', *A&U*, no. 11/194 (1986), p. 21-156.

Martin Pawley, 'Da Londra. Palumbo ci prova ancora', *Casabella*, vol. 50, no. 528 (1986), p. 40-41.

[Album]

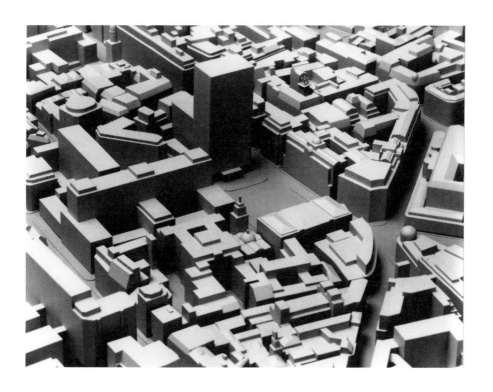

Colin Morris Associates, Model of Mies van der Rohe's
Mansion House project in context, 1981,
photograph by John Donat [RIBA Collections]

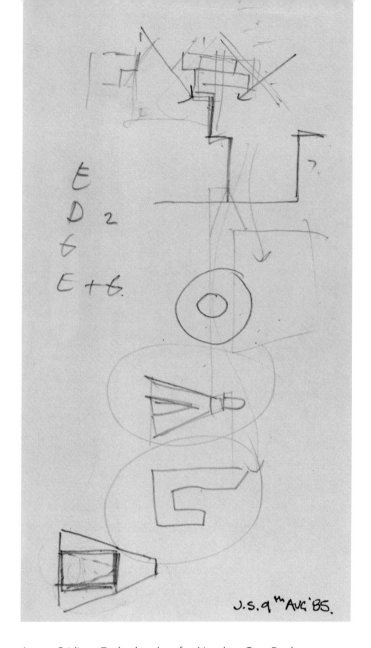

James Stirling, Early sketches for Number One Poultry,
9 August 1985, pencil on the back of an envelope

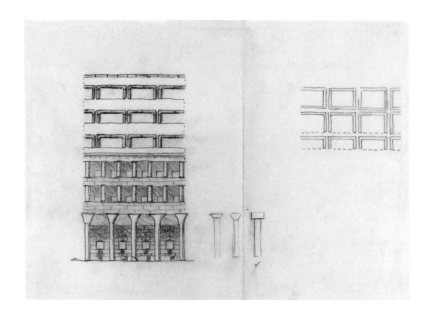

James Stirling, Study sketches for the elevations,
circa 1985, pencil and coloured pencils on tracing paper

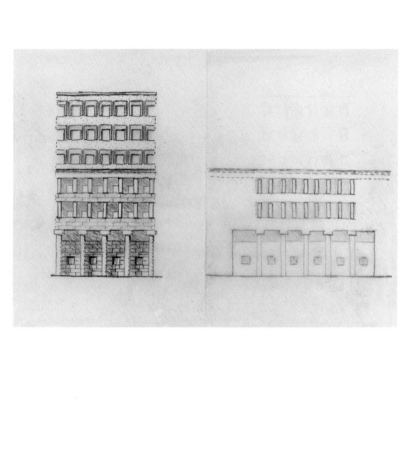

James Stirling, Sketches of scheme A, retaining the Mappin & Webb building, November 1985, pencil on tracing paper

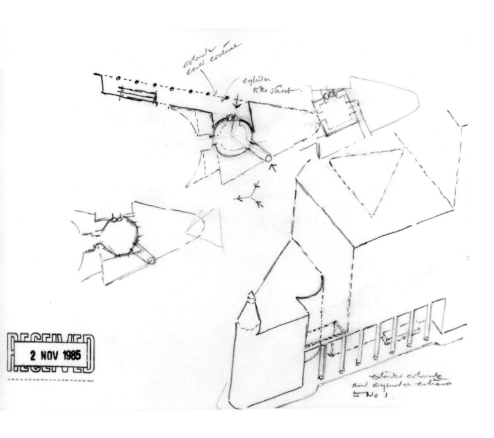

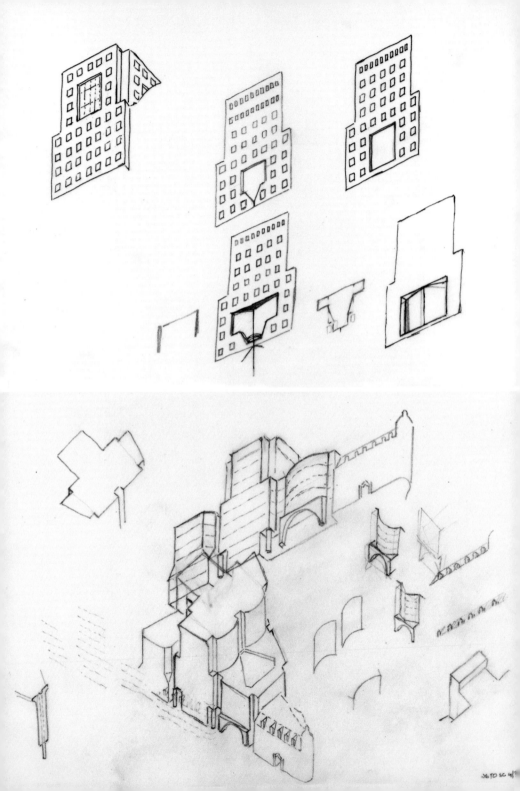

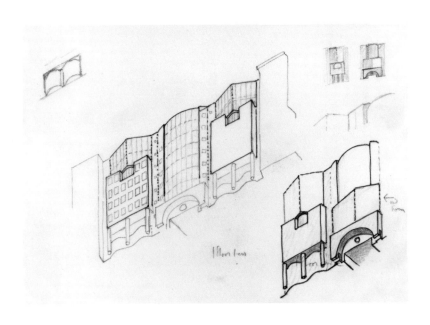

Left: James Stirling, Worm's eye views and axonometric with details
of the façades and of the fenestrations, Scheme A, 1985-86,
pencil and pen on tracing paper.
James Stirling, Worm's eye views of the façades, Scheme B, 1986,
pencil, coloured pencil and pen on tracing paper.

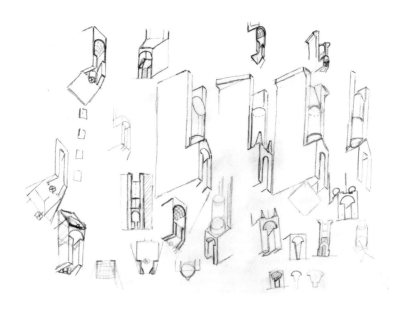

James Stirling, Sketches for corner entrance, circa 1986,
pencil on tracing paper.
Right: James Stirling, Worm's eye view of corner elevation, 1986-87,
crayon and red pen notes on print

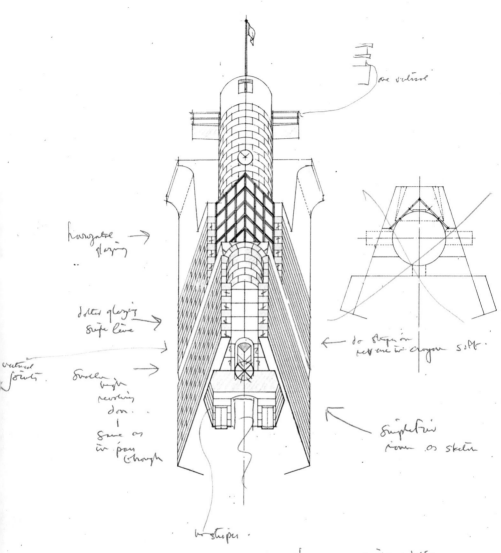

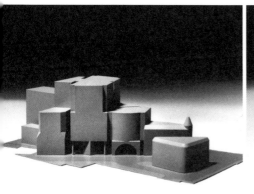

On this and the following page:
Colin Morris Associates, Models of Number One Poultry projects.
Left image: scheme A; right image: scheme B, 1:1250, 1986-88,
photographs by John Donat [RIBA Collections]

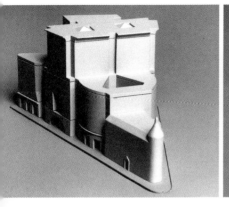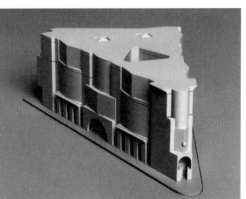

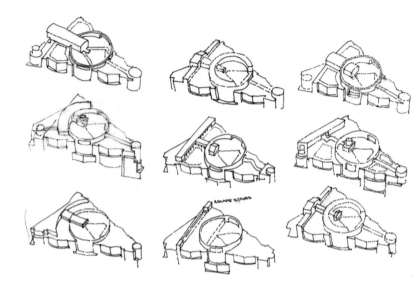

James Stirling, Michael Wilford and Associates,
Alternative designs for the roof, 1987, pen on tracing paper.
Right: Colin Morris Associates, Models of alternative designs for the roof,
circa 1988, photographs by John Donat [RIBA Collections]

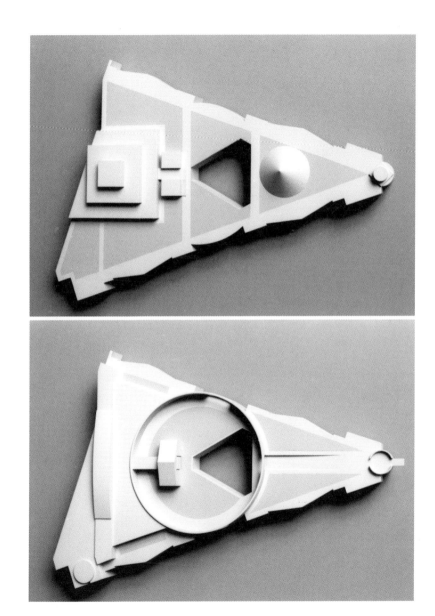

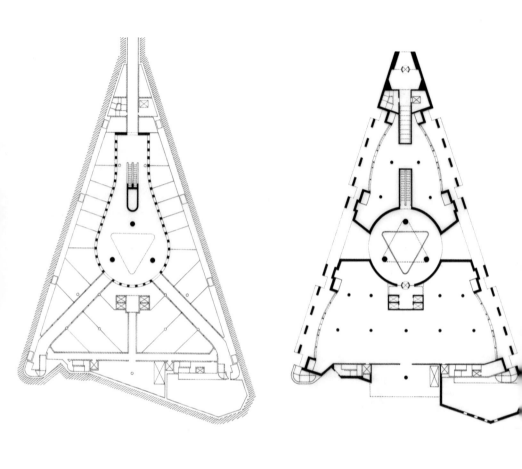

James Stirling, Michael Wilford and Associates, Preliminary plans
of concourse, ground Floor and roof, 1988, ink on tracing paper

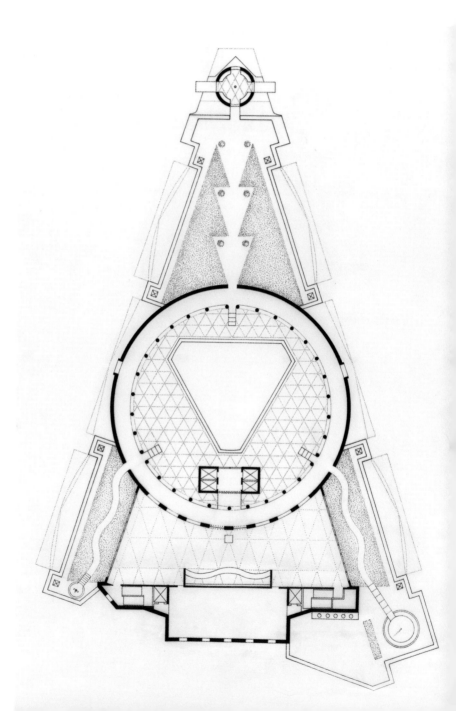

James Stirling, Michael Wilford and Associates,
View from Cornhill, May 1988, ink on tracing paper

VIEW FROM CORNHILL   VP-4   SHOWN WITH BOLSA HOUSE REVISED
SCHEME SEPT '86

STIRLING WILFORD & ASSOC   MAY 88

James Stirling, Michael Wilford and Associates,
View from Cornhill, May 1988, ink on tracing paper.
Right: James Stirling, Michael Wilford and Associates,
Perspective from Bank, circa 1988, ink on tracing paper.
Next page: James Stirling, Michael Wilford and Associates,
Detail Drawing, 3 September 1993, ink on tracing paper

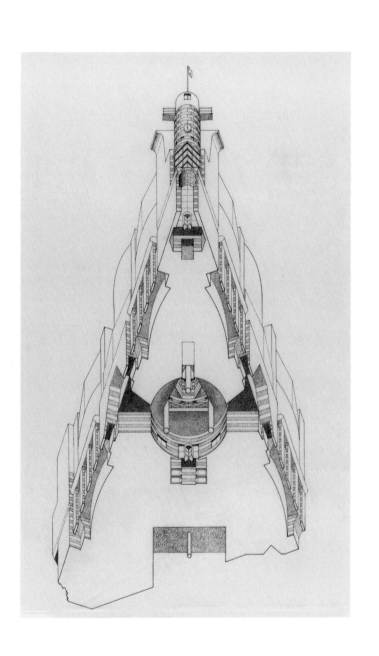

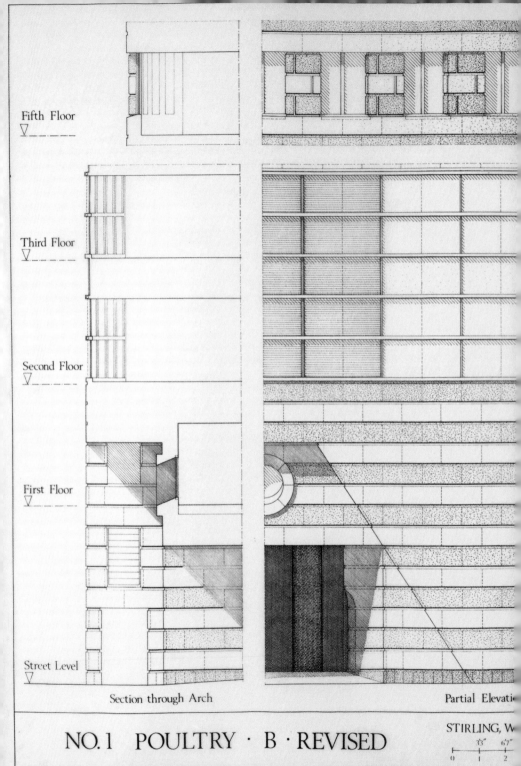

Fifth Floor ▽

Third Floor ▽

Second Floor ▽

First Floor ▽

Street Level ▽

Section through Arch

Partial Elevati

NO.1 POULTRY · B · REVISED

STIRLING, W

33″   67″

0   1   2

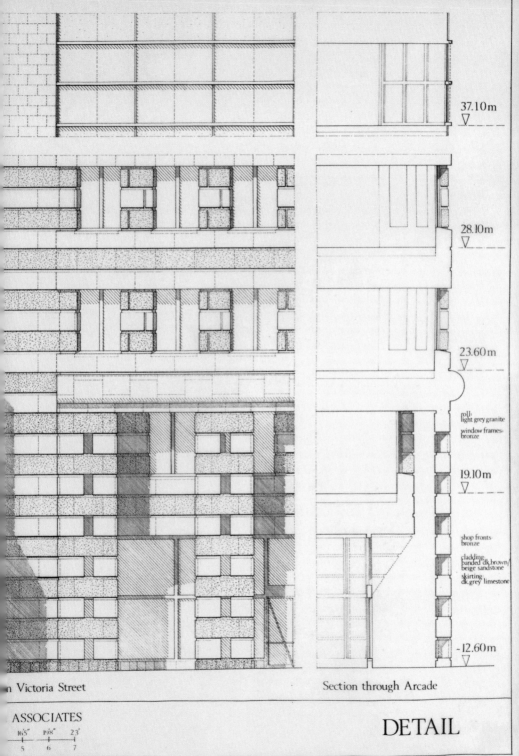

roll,
light grey granite

window frames,
bronze

37.10m
▽

28.10m
▽

23.60m
▽

19.10m
▽

shop fronts,
bronze

cladding,
banded dk.brown/
beige sandstone

skirting,
dk.grey limestone

~12.60m
▽

n Victoria Street

Section through Arcade

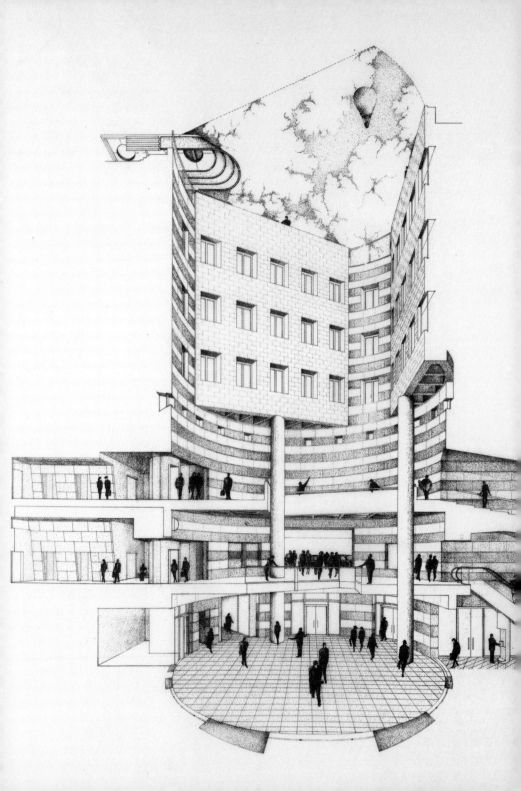

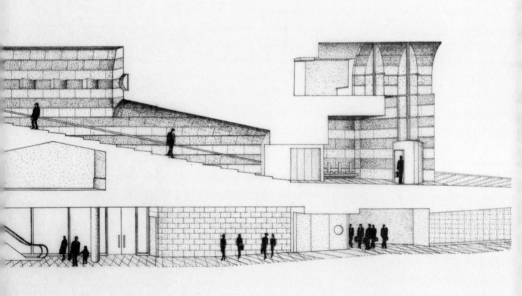

Previous pages: Michael Wilford and Partners,
Sectional perspective of Number One Poultry, 1994, ink on tracing paper.
Right and following pages: Richard Bryant, aerial view; internal courtyard,
Queen Victoria Street façade and detail of the corner, 1997, photoprints

[Correspondence]

Twentieth Century Society
11 June 2015

Significance
The Casework Committee considered this building to be of very high special interest. This is due to the pre-eminence of the architect Sir James Stirling, the innovative nature of the design and the high quality of the materials and execution. The very prominent site in the heart of the City also has an interesting and controversial history of redevelopment, which adds to its historic interest. No.1 Poultry is one of London's most striking buildings and a major work in Stirling's oeuvre. The building remains remarkably intact, with the only notable additions the insertion of later partitions on the first and second floors.

In Charles Jencks' book, *The New Paradigm in Architecture*, the author states that "No. 1 Poultry, replacing one of the last Victorian office clusters, took up medieval street patterns, a surrounding Classical grammar, the morphology of a triangular, corner site, and combined aspects of these contrasting forces with the requirements of a modern office block. Beyond this the building provided a roof garden and a circular, public realm off set from the street in a dense part of London where such open space is most welcome. The resultant grammar is a syncopated hybrid playing a checkerboard theme: large windowed offices step back and forth above large volumes of banded masonry also stepping up and down. But the syncopation of these big sections break down the scale in a way that is far superior to the continuous monoliths of Lutyens, Baker and the Classicists around it. Stirling, perhaps learning a lesson from Léon Krier who was in his office 15 years previously, shows how the multinational office leviathan can be heterogeneous and grammatical" (*The New Paradigm in Architecture: the Language of Postmodernism*, by Charles Jencks, p. 178).

The *Architectural Review* also praised the building's "intelligence and spatial complexity": "As No. 1 Poultry bursts into view like a peachy rainbow as you drive up Cornhill […]. It's still a strange thing to look at, almost ridiculous in its colour and verging on cartoon in its formalism, the building's apparent dumbness bristles with interlocking denseness and determined engagement with its urban context. Its combination of stupidity and obviousness with intelligence and spatial complexity makes the architecture that surrounds it - both context and contemporaneous - seem dumber, meaner and duller" (*Architectural Review*, March 2011, 'Situating Stirling: Five viewpoints', by Sam Jacob).

There is no doubt that that No. 1 Poultry is one of the most outstanding examples of post-modern architecture in London, if not the United Kingdom. The Society has taken a strong in interest in the building, and it featured in our recent book, *100 Buildings for 100 Years*, published last year by Batsford Publishing. Members of the committee considered that proposals for major alterations should be viewed in this context.

Twentieth Century Society Comment
The Casework Committee felt very strongly that any approach to significant change should recognise the architectural grandeur and monumentality of this building, as well as key intellectual strategies of apparent "stupidity" and "syncopation" as commented on by the critics mentioned above. Members considered that the alterations to the external envelope of No.1 Poultry, as currently proposed, risked harming the significance of the building by irreversibly changing the relationship between solids and voids on the road elevations. […]

Remit: The Twentieth Century Society was founded in 1979 and is the national amenity society concerned with the protection, appreciation, and study of post-1914 architecture, townscape and design. The Society is acknowledged in national planning guidance as the key organisation concerned with the modern period and is a constituent member of the Joint Committee of the National Amenity Societies. Under the procedures set out in *ODPM Circular 09/2005*, all English local planning authorities must inform the Twentieth Century Society when an application for listed building consent involving partial or total demolition is received, and they must notify us of the decisions taken on these applications.

Andrew Birds, Richard Portchmouth and Mike Russum
19 June 2015

Andrew Birds, Richard Portchmouth & Mike Russum are former employees of James Stirling and worked at JSMWA from 1981 to 1989 prior to setting up our practice Birds Portchmouth Russum Architects (BPR) in 1989. We all worked on No. 1 Poultry for a period when the project was going through the planning stages. Specifically, we had a significant role in the design development and preparing the presentation drawings and models for the Public Inquiry. Richard Portchmouth was responsible for producing six agreed views, which were a key focus of the discussion at the Public Inquiry.

During the period of design development, we explored in great detail the composition of the façades to Queen Victoria Street, Poultry & Royal Exchange. These façades were all conceived to respond to their formal civic context. This included the three dimensional sculptural quality of the elevations, fastidiously examined through upview and down view axonometrics – drawings which are synonymous with Jim Stirling's formula for creating masterpiece buildings. Importantly these drawings were used as a tool to develop the public realm within the colonnades and circular courtyard pass-through. A particular reference for Jim was Hawksmoor's St Mary Woolnoth where the extraordinary horizontal banding on the portico is echoed in the base to No. 1 Poultry. The depth of the porticos and the sculptural quality they give to the overall modelling of the building to bring it to rest comfortably in its context is critical to the overall composition. [...]

Similarly, the proportions of the internal rotunda were carefully conceived to create a comfortable composition of solid to void from the base to top of the building and these are balanced with the external window proportions so that the rotunda reads as a "cut out" element within the urban block. The proposal to introduce new and larger openings on the internal rotunda façade would destroy this carefully conceived relationship.

1 Poultry is a hugely significant building from one of the world's leading architects at the time and a project that represents the shift in urban modern architecture from object to contextual buildings. The building is an important addition to the collection of architectural set pieces at Bank junction. Any proposals for change need to be put forward with an approach, which is in absolute sympathy with the principles, which make this an outstanding building. The current proposals do not achieve this, are not satisfactory and should be rejected.

Simon Usher
21 June 2015

I worked at the offices of Michael Wilford and Partners from 1993 to 2000. I was specifically employed to work on No.1 Poultry (from 1993 to 1996). I principally worked with another architect, Paul Barke (now Barke-Asuni) and together we produced the drawings and specification for the main contractor tenders. We both continued to work on the project throughout the construction period - with our aim that the quality of the detailing and craftsmanship of the execution of the build would reflect the quality of the Stirling design, befitting the stature of the design and its unique context at Bank. The selection of materials and the details were developed in a very careful and exacting manner.

Of fundamental importance to the Stirling design are the three dimensional, layered and sculpted façades to Poultry and Queen Victoria Street which respond to scale and nature of the formal civic context; Mansion House, the Royal Exchange, the Bank of England and the Midland Bank - the buildings which form the unique architectural composition that is Bank. No.1 Poultry now contributes to and is part of that composition. […] Essential to the principle façades of Poultry are the free standing 2 storey columns, clad in intermittent bands of yellow stone from Toowoomba, Australia and Wilderness red from Gloucestershire, which enclose the public arcade behind. […]

The principle façades comprise 3 bays of modulated elements divided by 4 stone clad vertical cores. Although not perhaps immediately apparent to most observers the sculptural forms of the façade are made possible by a tour de force of structural engineering. It is of significance that the first floor façade (behind the columns) are formed by huge concrete Vierendeel beams that span from core to core. The openings in the Vierendeel beam form the windows to the first floor offices and the beam provides a column free glazed façade to the shops at ground level. […]

However, at the time the building was completed the red sandstone quarry had effectively been "run dry" in terms of the scale of stone that was available for No.1 Poultry. The stone from Australia may be available, however, the beds in the quarry that are currently being worked may not produce stone that matches the stone on the building. It is of note that every slab of the Australian stone was subjected to careful selection in Italy before it was allowed to be carved and fixed onto the building. […]

I consider that No.1 Poultry is of critical importance in the sequential development of architecture in Britain and as such I support the proposal for the building to be listed and thereby preventing architectural adulteration.

Clive Atkinson
24 June 2015

As an original member of the design team working for Arup in their newly formed Façade Engineering Team I had the unique opportunity of working on the One Poultry project. The Stirling Wilford and Partners team developed their design using beautifully crafted hand drawn sketches and the to and fro dialogue between the Arup and architectural design team fuelled innovation and advanced cladding concepts, creating a new relationship between the Architect and Engineer.

The detailing of the main sandstone façade was reminiscent of Stirling's Staatsgalerie and follows its open joint rainscreen aesthetic but was additionally accented with closed joint cavity wall. The design dictated very sharp edges and returns so we developed details that would allow stone returns without trims or copings, with water management at cills using concealed gutters and downpipes; at parapets using a carefully designed coping detail that managed water. These details have allowed the building to have a largely stain-free stone surface.

Selection of the stone, with a global search resulting in the Arup architectural geologists sourcing a relatively unknown stone from Brisbane Australia and a more locally sourced English stone for the project, rejecting Scottish and South African stones along the way on technical grounds. The figured Brisbane sandstone (Helidon) was matched against a red sandstone from Gloucestershire (Wilderness Red); the stone sizes were at the limit of the Gloucester quarries bed and Poultry eventually exhausted the quarry – whilst the beige sandstone was sourced to have a similar level of figuration as the Staatsgalerie. As the project featured open joints the Arup team undertook an extensive study to determine suitability, including checking joint dimension against native avian species.

The stone and window relationship was extremely significant and each window was meticulously set out according to the outer alignment, the planning grid and the curve; resulting in some acute reveals and edges; these were deliberate and faithful to the Stirling design so were preserved at all costs. From my experience during construction removing and/or repositioning stones and achieving a sealed weather-tight joint around any new window and door openings will be technically very problematic, and may result in a marked change to the current finished details.

The bronze shop front windows were also all curved despite their shallow radius, a highly expensive option that was developed to maintain the quality of the design. […]

The setting of the stone back from the street to form a colonnade was once described to me as Stirling's interpretation of the massive order of classical architecture (Jim talked about the high game of Architecture) and was borne in the spirit of other buildings facing the Bank interchange at Mansion House Square, including buildings by Edwin Lutyens, Herbert Baker (after John Soane), George Dance the Elder and William Tite. These free standing elements offer a civic presence to the building that contemporary buildings rarely offer and are a treasured reference to the importance of the building and its location. Indeed, there are many references to this classical order including the granite clad bull nosed pediments that top the columns, the curved Doric bell motif towards the prow of Mansion House Square and the castellated turret in stone and bronze.

The ground level bronze faced shop fronts were manufactured by a Birmingham based shop fitters who developed the façades using their hand crafted approach; creating 1:1 pencil drawings. Following faithfully the Stirling design the large curved glass shop fronts were the biggest pieces of curved glass installed in the UK at that time and were not without laboured design discussion. [...]

Double skin curtain walling to triangulated façades – used for energy and acoustic performance; a very early deliberate attempt to control the solar gains and road traffic noise to the façades. The façades were also double height yet retained a single transom floor separation – the detail was the first use of a fire engineered separation detail to achieve a high fire compartment performance.

The clock facing Bank is set into and is supported by the glass – it took four attempts to get this double glazed unit and frame onto the building in one piece – due to its size and weight. The clock mechanism sits on a bevel in the glass unit and the hour points were supported off the perimeter frame. Access is from an inner skin of glass that opens like a butterfly to gain access to the electric clock.

The listed terracotta frieze to the north façade originally came off

No. 13 Poultry. The frieze represents a parade of Queen Elizabeth I through London and was originally vertically aligned – after much discussion with the City and English Heritage it was agreed to lay them out in parade order. […]

The faience glazed courtyard panels with coloured reveals to the atrium were not an original concept; with Stirling inspired up-views showing stone as the early design aspiration. I have only recently discovered that the faience is a reference to the many City court-yards that have ceramic tiling, Stirling was known to have liked this and the 1994 review introduced the coloured faience feature. The faience was sourced for its colour (they were deliberately not white as daylight distribution in such a large courtyard was not neces-sary), the dark colour of the faience offsets the coloured reveals of the openings that would have been less effective had a stone façade been used and I believe enhances the space and sets the composition to the office and restaurant entrances and the roof level lift housing. The faience panels were the largest available at the time. The cills for these windows and the lower edges of the faience capture and drain to the central columns so that there are few drips onto the public. Where the stone is used to unify the de-sign in the curved corners there are also curved windows. The atrium is now a treasured space that was donated to the City at a time when similar public spaces and cross routes were and have since continued to be lost.

Case for listing
The building is a unique example of James Stirling's work and cer-tainly emblematic of its time and demonstrated a design of Stirling at his architectural maturity. The rigid geometric pattern was played out in full and the attention to Stirling's vision, even after his death, was always at the forefront of design decisions. I will be very disap-pointed if the building is significantly changed as the nation will lose something quite special. […]

Charles Jencks
26 June 2015

As someone closely involved with the history of Number One Poultry from its inception, I would like to make several comments as an architectural historian about its value, especially from a Post-Modern perspective where it occupies a key place in British history.

First, the suggestion that the design was somehow altered after Stirling's death, or didn't reflect his ideas in detail, is easily dismissed. There was an in-depth Public Inquiry before his demise which examined his intentions at great length and in minute detail. The transcripts themselves are a significant monument of the debate at the time – on history, contextualism, scale, symbolism and function. This historic battle deserves publication, as important as the 14th century debate between the French and Italian architects about Milan cathedral.

The building, and debate, illustrate some core values of post-modern urbanism. Among them is the value of contextualism that not only acknowledges the adjacent buildings in scale and material, but also shows that contrast is essential for meaning to be communicated. Thus large urban volumes are broken up into syncopated areas of glass and masonry; banded horizontals are contrasted with vertical breaks; foreground with background; and the quiet, interior piazza gains meaning versus the noisy cylindrical tower. The last symbolically marks "Ground Zero for the City, the busiest corner in Britain."

Such contrasts, and musical syncopations of the highest order, make this building one of the three British urban landmarks of its time. Along with the extension to the National Gallery and 30 St Mary's Axe (aka The Gherkin), it epitomises the iconic and communicational motives of that period.

Developers want to push out the "glazing line to the portico columns" and call the recessive windows "misaligned" with these "columns" (actually piers) - a bit like saying Stravinsky's rhythms and syncopations in *The Rite of Spring* are out of step with each other and should be lined up and regularised. There are much less invasive ways of getting more light and advertisement into these spaces than destroying the spaces and fabric of this masterpiece.

The building was finished - 1998 - when Post-Modernism was unfashionable, but I believe it is a superb essay in that kind of urbanism, will be respected and loved in the future, and is easily (along with Hawksmoor's and Wren's work nearby) among the best architecture of its type in the City.

Darren Stewart Capel
26 June 2016

[…] No.1 Poultry is often misunderstood as being an expression of personal sentiments, but actually it is a learned expression of contemporary and traditional themes. The architectural composition was designed after Stirling carefully considered the context of fine works of architecture and the space that unites them. No.1 Poultry is imbued with reference, reflection and resonance to Midland Bank, St Mary Woolnoth, Mansion House, Bank of England and even Lloyds. By interweaving modern and ancient, reworking and revitalizing tradition with contemporary potential, James Stirling created an architecture reverberant of the morphological continuum of a historic city. At No.1 Poultry James Stirling expressed the contemporary culture in a way that was new and apposite to the age yet it embodied the English intellectual culture of reinterpreting and reinvigorating traditional forms in an attempt to create an ennobling frame for the daily work and spiritual contemplation of modern life. […]

James Stirling was undoubtedly an individual talent for architecture: thinking, drawing and building within the British tradition. In 1919 T.S. Eliot wrote in his celebrated essay 'Tradition and the

Individual Talent' (I have transposed the familiar excerpt in terms of architecture rather than poetry): "Tradition cannot be inherited, and if you want it you must obtain it by great labour. It involves in the first place, the historical sense, which involves a perception, not only of the pastness of the past, but of its presence; and compels an architect to work not merely with his own generation in his bones, but with a feeling that the whole of the architecture from Imhotep and within it the whole of the architecture of his own country has a simultaneous existence and composes a simultaneous order. This historical sense, which is a sense of the timeless as well as the temporal, is what makes an architect traditional. And it is at the same time that what makes an architect most acutely conscious of his place in time, of his own contemporaneity."

Time is required for all that develops and crystallizes in our world of thoughts, and perhaps architecture needs more time than any other art, but often works of architecture, such as James Stirling's No.1 Poultry are threatened before enough times has passed for their significant quality to be appreciated widely. [...] In the interests of the City of London and the Nation, No.1 Poultry should be listed.

James Stirling was the British architect that is most synonymous with Post-Modernism and No.1 Poultry is the most eloquent expression of those ideas that was built in Britain. In 1980 James Stirling was honoured with the RIBA Gold Medal, and Pritzker Prize Laureate in 1981, with the jury citation stating: "We honor James Stirling - a prodigy for so many years - as a leader of the great transition from the Modern Movement to the architecture of the New - an architecture that once more has recognized historical roots, once more has close connections with the buildings surrounding it, once more can be called a new tradition. Originality within this tradition is Stirling's distinction." [...]

Michael Wilford, Laurence Bain, Russell Bevington
29 June 2015

[…] 1 Poultry reinterprets and reinforces the significance, history and geometry of its location, whilst satisfying a commercial brief for an office development at the heart of the City. It is an efficient building, developed through rigorous analysis of the constraints of the triangular site and the application of clear architectural principles and ideas. […]

From the start of our involvement the Chief Planning Officer described to us his vision of a City where buildings strike a balance between commercial considerations and obligation to the public realm. We very much took this vision to heart when firstly developing the concept then detailing and constructing 1 Poultry.

The design was intensively scrutinised through a very public Planning Inquiry in 1988 when James Stirling explained every detail of the proposals, using very accurate drawings, models, material samples and a multitude of planning, commercial agents and engineering reports. Our proposals were approved by the Secretary of State in 1989 and the legal hurdles were cleared finally in the House of Lords in 1991 shortly before James Stirling's death in 1992.

From 1992 onwards all the members of our design team followed the accurate drawings and detailed description produced for the Inquiry. As a team we working closely with the commercial agents to maximise the financial returns, with Ove Arup Engineers to detail the building, with EC Harris on the construction budget and Montagu Evans to obtain all planning, road closure and other approvals. All this was done without compromising the approved design.

During the design development and construction process we very much appreciated the commitment and guidance of Peter Rees and his colleagues in their scrutiny of our drawings and regular on site inspections.

We cannot fathom the reasons why such radical changes which ignore totally the concept that has worked so well are being proposed and fear that if consent were to be given further "refurbishments" would quickly follow.

We ask that the Application is rejected and that the Applicants be advised that the City will not entertain any future applications that are disrespectful of the design and the setting of the buildings in the Conservation Area.

Zaha Hadid
30 June 2015

I am writing to strongly object to the recently submitted planning application to alter 1 Poultry.

The building designed by Sir James Stirling is a post-modernist masterpiece that deserves to be kept as a monument to innovative design and excellent execution.

Any suggestions that the building is not as James intended are spurious and can be easily proven untrue by Laurence Bain; who has the the original concept design drawings, various beautiful hand drawn presentation drawings and all the production information which can be produced if necessary. […]

This iconic site in the heart of the city is one of London's most striking projects and deserves a Grade II listing status. We must surely all do our utmost to ensure that we do not destroy yet another beautiful example of post-modernist architecture.

No. 1 Poultry deserves to be saved due to its architectural elegance and innovation; demolishing parts of such an iconic building would be a deeply regrettably mistake.

Piers Gough
1 July 2015

James Stirling was one of the great internationally renowned architects of the 20th Century. He was in a long British mannerist tradition which included Vanbrugh, Hawksmoor, Soane and Lutyens. No. 1 Poultry is one of only a handful of new buildings by him completed in England. It is the perfect example of his later work.

Commissioned by an enlightened and generous patron of art and architecture Peter Palumbo, Stirling was able to conceive of a complex masterpiece that was not constrained in its representation of the City. It is a masterful expression of London's place at the centre of global finance and the modern city of complex restless money dealing which has replaced the historic neoclassical certainty or more modern pinstripe architecture of the banking square mile.

The building offered a generous public realm to the constrained pavements of the area in contrast to the surrounding hermetic palazzos. It is this public realm which is presently under threat of removal/ alteration by current appallingly ill-conceived proposals.

Jim Stirling was a master of the art of architecture. He was consummate in the combination of historical reference with the most modern of building materials and techniques. This three dimensional complexity and richness of iconography are unique in the Post Modern canon. No. 1 Poultry embodies all these qualities. It should receive the protection afforded to neighbouring masterpieces such as St Mary Woolnooth, The Bank of England, Royal Exchange, Mansion House and Midland Bank, and remain a complete work as conceived and built.

I trust your department will urgently consider listing it in Grade I.

Norman Foster
7 July 2015

I would like to add my voice to the growing chorus of rightful opposition to the proposed changes to No. 1 Poultry, which was designed by James Stirling and is located at the very heart of the City of London.

This is the work of a commission by one of the great patrons of architecture, Lord Palumbo, and one of the most outstanding and influential architects of his generation on the world stage.

The work is overdue for protection either by listing or a clear rejection of the proposed changes.

Siegfried Wernik
8 July 2015

I was the Associate and head of the Stuttgart office of James Stirling, Michael Wilford and Partners from 1979 until 1990.

Many academics and architectural commentators consider the State Gallery (Staatsgalerie) in Stuttgart to be one of the most important buildings of the 20th century. The Staatsgalerie Stuttgart, including the New Chamber Theatre, has been listed in 2014 with the highest category for monument buildings in Baden-Wüttemberg.

Some suggest that there are strong connections between the design of Number One Poultry and the State Gallery. Indeed, the Planning Inspector in his report of the 1998 inquiry wrote: "If there are recollections of other recent Stirling designs that is not surprising given that the same mind has been brought to bear on each of those problems. What is in my opinion singularly impressive about the coherence of this design is the way in which the central unifying feature - the drum - is pre-echoed in the curves of the ground floor shop fronts and of the parts of the office floors," the Inspector added, "if the drum were to prove anything like the successful public attraction of the drum at the Neue Staatsgalerie in Stuttgart it would serve its purpose well."

Why would anyone consider altering in anyway the very parts of the design which the Inspector highlighted? Would anyone even contemplate similar changes to the Staatsgalerie? They would be the subject in Stuttgart and other parts of Germany of ridicule. Not only this, alterations to the Staatsgalerie cannot be made to that extent, since the building is already listed as unique monument.

Changes to Number One Poultry would devalue what is a very interesting "conversation" between the two buildings in two countries.

Mary Stirling
9 July 2015

My husband's great care and concern for this building and his involvement on the design process at all levels is well recorded.

As unique example of his late work, any modification should sensitively preserve the building. Some updating may be necessary after 17 years, but any changes, while obviously aimed at engaging the current needs of tenants, should also (and most importantly) preserve the building's long term integrity and the existing quality of the environment. […]

In my view the current proposals emasculate the design concept.

In this connection, may I suggest you refer to the attached quotation from Ada Louise Huxtable, the eminent American critic, writing about my husband's conceptual integrity.

I do hope you will bear these considerations in mind. […]

The strength of Stirling's best work derives from his conceptual visualization of a building not as of conventionally linked separate rooms or spaces, but as a totality, an immediate whole, understood instantly and in all of its parts and relationships. This gives his work enormous resonance. Whatever his sources and however he used them, Stirling's exceptional vision was of a unified object in space and time. This brilliant conceptual synthesis, with its powerful spatial relationships, is the hallmark of truly great architecture – the single, consistent, enduring and timeless feature that separates the masters from the dilettantes and decorators.

Edward Jones
10 July 2015

As an observer of London over the past three decades, recorded in *Guide to the Architecture of London*, with my coauthor Christopher Woodward, I have become aware that there are very few post war office buildings that make successful public realm contributions. The office building as a type has a tendency to privatize city land. Here at No. 1 Poultry, the Rotunda and Colonnades generously give space to those entering or leaving Bank station and also provides much needed elbow room and a short cut at at this congested intersection. [...] In the commercial philistinism of the present one is almost nervous to mention that in addition these considerable urban design attributes, No. 1 Poultry is also a significant and mature work of one of Britain's most celebrated Architects. We note in our section on the City: "At this important intersection Stirling took his (justifiable) place in a small pantheon of English Architects; Lutyens, Soane, Hawksmoor, Dance and Wren."

It should not go unnoticed that Soane's marvelous banking halls opposite were scandalously demolished to make way for the unfortunate Herbert Baker's additions to the Bank of England. As Wilde might have observed for this to happen once is a misfortune but for it to happen twice at the same intersection "looks like carelessness."

Colin Morris
12 July 2015

I have been involved with this site since the early 1980s, firstly working with Peter Carter, the project architect tasked with following through the Mies van der Rohe proposals, and later I was to work closely with James Stirling on his designs for the Number One Poultry project.

Both Peter Carter and James Stirling were unique architects who shared extremely exacting standards, as they sought the ultimate in every detail in respect of their designs, which had to be "just right" - errors were simply not tolerated. Throughout the years of design development, we built numerous architectural models for Stirling.

Firstly, we were asked to build a context model at scale 1:1250 of the whole of the Bank area. All the buildings that surrounded the site were faithfully built to microscopic detail and accuracy. As I distinctly recall, Stirling wanted to analyse and understand the whole area - the surrounding listed buildings and the street patterns in the Conservation Area.

Secondly, we built a series of over a dozen models for the One Poultry site which could be slotted into the context model. To start with there were two options - scheme A which retained the Mappin and Webb building and scheme B which developed the whole site. There were then several development models of each scheme. When a model was completed I hastily took it over to the offices at 8 Fitzroy Square. Stirling would first examine the latest development model and then carefully slot it into the context model, holding it up to the light and with one eye look down each street.

If, and that was a big if, Jim was happy with the small scale model he would then ask for a 1:500 scale model to be built - these were more detailed, but deliberately did not include windows. He explained that he was firstly interested in getting the geometry right, then windows would be added and then stonework - it was a layered approach.

I recall that our models were on display at the Public Exhibition and at the Public Inquiry where they were examined and commented on by all sides – to the best of my knowledge no one found any errors or contested their accuracy. The building we see today looks exactly like the final scale 1:1250 and uncannily indistinguishable to 1:500 models that we built. Jim Stirling demanded perfection and I believe that is what he got from the models we faithfully detailed and engineered. [...]

George A. Hayes
13 July 2015

[...] The buildings designed by James Stirling are classical: he avoided the clichés of Modernism and continued the tradition of past ages. Please remember that nothing can be added or taken away from a classic. The listing of No. 1 Poultry is imperative!

Richard Rogers
13 July 2015

I am writing to strongly object to the recently submitted planning application to alter One Poultry.

James Stirling was the first British architect to develop a truly modern style. One Poultry is a beautiful designed, post-modern masterpiece which fits neatly into its prominent site. It is one of his last buildings and pays special attention to the context, use of materials and subtle playfulness.

Because the building will not reach 30 years of age until 2024, it needs to be listed at grade II*. In my opinion, this is an excellent example of post-modernist architecture, and does deserve this level of recognition. If it were to be demolished, or altered as currently proposed – would be deeply regrettable.

Mark Swenarton
13 July 2015

I am writing to object to the above application. It would make damaging changes to one of the most important buildings constructed in the City of London in the past 50 years and a major work by the most important British architect of the second half of the twentieth century.

Number One Poultry was the result of an exhaustive planning process, including a Public Inquiry and an appeal to the High Court, extending over a period of ten years following the rejection of the previous proposal, and was designed with the support of, and in close collaboration with, the City planning authorities and in particular the chief planner Mr Peter Rees. The goal was to demonstrate how the commercial requirements of the owner and occupants could be reconciled with the interests of the wider community in the City, to produce a building that enhances daily life in the City by the way that it sits within, and maintains pedestrian routes across and alongside, its apex-shaped site.

This site is one of the most important in the City of London: *The Heart of the Empire* as portrayed by the artist Niels Moller Lund in his 1904 painting of that name. It was in recognition of this importance that the building was designed by James Stirling, his partner Michael Wilford and their team in the years from 1985 to 1994.

Neighbours of Number One Poultry include masterpieces by some of the greatest names in British architecture, including Hawksmoor (St Mary Woolnooth), Soane (Bank of England), Dance (Mansion House) and Lutyens (Midland Bank). Alongside these James Stirling's Number One Poultry ranks as a worthy equal.

James Stirling is recognized worldwide as the greatest architect of the second half of the twentieth century in Britain and, some would say, in the world.

In the past five years no fewer than six major books on Stirling have been published in the USA and UK (Vidler 2010, Berman 2010, Baker 2011, Crinson 2012, Reeser Lawrence 2012 and Berman 2015), while there have also been themed issues of architectural journals devoted to Stirling, from The Netherlands (Oase 2009) to Japan (JA+U 2015). Such is the esteem in which this exceptional architect is held.

Number One Poultry is the largest and most complex project built by Stirling in London and as such its importance cannot be over-estimated. It would be an act of appalling barbarism to allow it to be damaged heedlessly and as such would bring international op-probrium on the City of London. I trust therefore that this applica-tion will be turned down.

Simon Nurney
24 July 2015

[...] I know the No.1 project very well and I am very familiar with all the depth and rigour that the architectural team applied throughout the design and construction process. In my opinion, the building is an exceptional example of the work of Sir James Stirling.

It is, as the Inspector predicted at the time, a "masterpiece" of late twentieth century architecture and, in reality, it is also far more than a purely commercial building.

The public's ability to explore and enjoy the views of the City as well as the building's fascinating architectural details from the concourse level, along the ground floor colonnades and through the Bucklers-bury Passage as well as up to the roof garden makes this building almost unique within the City of London.

Every time that I visit the building I find something new in the fasci-nating geometry of the spaces. [...]

Paul Barke-Asuni
4 February 2016

[…] As an architect who was involved with the design in the James Stirling Michael Wilford and Associates (JSMWA) office from the start and later returned to complete the job I can unequivocally state that this is a Stirling building. And I would thank the City of London planners for helping us achieve this by their insistence that we followed the Stirling concept exactly. I would add that much has been made by those wishing to devalue the building and justify the changes suggest that this building is not a building by James Stirling but was a simulacrum completed some years after his death. Such is the nature of the architectural process that when an architect dies there may be a number of commissions outstanding. This was the case with the JSMWA Stuttgart Music School which was completed in 1997. I do not believe the authorship of this building has been questioned (either now or upon winning the Stirling prize) in the way No.1 Poultry has been questioned. Indeed, due to the scrutiny that the design of the latter was placed under at Public Inquiry it was a fully developed design at the time of Jim's death and we executed his design under the detailed scrutiny of the City Planners and English Heritage. There are numerous examples of buildings completed after the architect's death where the work is still attributed to the architect. The Church at Firminy Vert was started six years after the death of Le Corbusier and completed just ten years ago yet it is considered the work of Le Corbusier and not José Ouberie. The Barcelona Pavilion by Mies van De Rohe was destroyed in 1930 and rebuilt in 1986. It is not considered by those who gain enjoyment from it to be a piece of fakery. The work of Nicholas Hawksmoor to the West end of Westminster Abbey undertaken after his death and even the building of the houses of Parliament outlasted both Barry and Pugin. Such is the immense undertaking of architecture that in simple terms such things happen. No.1 Poultry was constructed and completed by those who knew Jim best, those like me who had worked with him for a number of years. […]

Terry Farrell
4 February 2016

I am writing to register my profound opposition to the tabled changes to James Stirling & Michael Wilford's Number One Poultry.

Like his seminal Neue Staatsgalerie in Stuttgart, Stirling's design has the public realm and pedestrian access at its heart. The colonnades, the central light well and the rooftop gardens are important expressions of civic openness at the centre of the country's often opaque banking district.

The generous covered space within the colonnade acts as both an important vehicle for increased capacity for the pavement, and as a powerful architectural expression on the façade that creates a sense of massiveness and solidity, demarcating a base for the overall composition.

The proposed changes would entirely undermine both the architectural effect, so vital to the balance of this complex design, and the practical benefits to the public realm. Similarly, the proposed new openings and increased window sizes are functionally unnecessary, and will undermine the viscerally sculptural forms of the building's interlocking geometries.

We are currently facing the loss, and wilfully destructive alteration, of much of our best postmodern architecture. Significant and hugely damaging changes presented as minor and based on tenant demands, are being allowed to undermine the architectural integrity of buildings that we must – with immediate urgency - begin protecting.

If these changes are allowed, Jim's vision and the integrity of a unique and virtuoso design realised in totality down to the smallest detail, will be lost forever.

Adam Nathaniel Furman
4 February 2016

Number One Poultry is the most perfect example in Britain, and possibly the world, of the postmodern style when turned to the creation of commercial buildings. Many were built with the style applied as a fashionable dressing to what were standard layouts behind the façade. Here James Stirling and Michael Wilford created a building that embodied the best of the period's preoccupations, in its every aspect. Like his Neue Staatsgalerie it is a design that has public access and permeation literally at its heart, with its central void, colonnades and roof gardens, treating these spaces as areas to be celebrated, with spectacular vistas and carefully articulated forms and beautiful material finishes greeting all who pass through it every day.

It is also a paragon of the postmodern preoccupation with the combination of multiple references, with the design simultaneously echoing a veritable menagerie of historical precedents, from rostral columns, ocean liners, and Egyptian temples, to classical palazzi, Louis Kahn, Le Corbusier and more. It is an incredibly evocative composition that is the perfect formal metaphor for the centre of a city whose most continuous quality in modern times has been its international status as the world's melting pot, of finance, cultures and communities. It achieves this "multivalence" while effortlessly attaining what Venturi described as the necessary "difficult whole", creating a forceful building that has an overall coherent presence, whilst being filled to the rafters with architectural references, details and delight.

The proposed changes to Number One Poultry will undermine what is the most complete and perfect realisation of James Stirling's vision of an architecture embedded in the city. Its importance lies in the totality of its parts all working together, and these changes - the enlarged windows where should be read the massiveness of pure geometry, the filling-in of the deep and high civic-scaled colonnades - will irrevocably damage this harmony. […]

[Listing]

Historic England

List entry summary
This building is listed under the Planning (Listed Buildings and Conservation Areas) Act 1990 as amended for its special architectural or historic interest.
Name: No.1 Poultry
List entry Number: 1428881

Location
1 Poultry, London, EC2R 8EJ
County: Greater London Authority
District: City and County of the City of London
District Type: London Borough
Parish: Non Civil Parish
National Park: Not applicable to this List entry.
Grade: II*
Date first listed: 28 November 2016
Date of most recent amendment: Not applicable to this List entry.

List entry description
Summary of building - Speculative commercial building incorporating offices and retail units, the Green Man public house, a public right of way in Bucklersbury Passage and rooftop restaurant and garden. Designed in 1985-88 by James Stirling, Michael Wilford and Associates for Peter Palumbo's City Acre Property Investment Trust Ltd, and built in 1994-98 by the practice, renamed Michael Wilford and Partners Ltd after Stirling's death in 1992.

Reasons for designation - No.1 Poultry, designed in 1985-88 by James Stirling, Michael Wilford and Associates, and built in 1994-98 by the practice, renamed Michael Wilford and Partners after Stirling's death in 1992, is listed at Grade II* for the following principal reasons:

*Architect: a highly significant late work by one of Britain's foremost post-war architects, which expresses Stirling's singular approach to design; *Architectural and design interest: an unsurpassed example of commercial post-modernism, on a monumental scale, intricate in its planning and rigorously scrutinised and executed; *Commercial development: one of the key developments of the post-war era, built by a prominent developer, determined to create a building of enduring quality; *Spatial interest and form: a striking symmetrical composition on a tightly constrained site, exemplifying Stirling's work in its exploration of space and movement though interlocking geometrical volumes and in its use of materials, colour and motifs, and exceptionally carrying this through to a dynamic interior space; *Planning: exemplary urban contextualism in a complex spatial inter-relationship of mixed-use office and retail accommodation, a public right of way, roof garden and restaurant, entrance to the underground station and public house, where the generosity of the public realm is exceptional for a speculative scheme; *Civic presence and group value: occupies a very prominent site in the heart of the City of London, in close proximity to highly prestigious civic and commercial buildings, which are referenced in the design.

History - Speculative commercial building incorporating offices and retail units, the Green Man pub and a rooftop restaurant and garden. Designed in 1985-88 by James Stirling, Michael Wilford and Associates for Peter Palumbo's City Acre Property Investment Trust Ltd, and built in 1994-98 by the practice, renamed Michael Wilford and Partners Ltd, after Stirling's death in 1992. In order to secure the project Palumbo entered into a joint venture with German financier Dieter Bock's company Advanta, and the project was managed by its subsidiary, Altstadtbau.

110

Planning history - The commission came from Lord Palumbo in July 1985 after an earlier scheme, designed by Mies van der Rohe in 1962-68, was rejected by the Secretary of State following Public Inquiry in 1984. The development was controversial from the outset given the prominence of the site within Bank Conservation Area, its proximity to highly graded listed buildings and in the demolition of Grade II listed buildings, notably Belcher's Mappin and Webb building, to secure the site. During 1986 two options were prepared, the first retaining the Mappin and Webb building, the second opting for total redevelopment. Following a second Public Inquiry in 1988, it was for the latter, Scheme B (Revised) that the Secretary for State, Nicholas Ridley, gave permission, seeing it as a potential masterpiece which was more important to the nation than the retention of the listed buildings. At the time a highly controversial development at the centre of a conservation battle, providing the catalyst for an important ideological debate, opponents of the scheme sought a judicial review which was overruled by the High Court, but it was not until 1991 that the House of Lords finally gave consent for the redevelopment to proceed. Once objections concerning the public right of way across the site were resolved, work finally began on site in 1994, concluding four years later.

Design - Stirling's design was developed in 1985-88, and in principle changed little thereafter. After Stirling's early death in 1992 the production of working drawings continued to be supervised by the practice (then Michael Wilford and Partners Ltd), with Laurence Bain as long-standing partner-in-charge of the project, and with Ove Arup and Partners continuing as engineers. The detailed design for No.1 Poultry was subject to particular scrutiny at Public Inquiry, by the High Court, the City planning authority and by English Heritage, and it was stipulated that it was to be built in accordance with the Secretary of State's decision. Intellectually powerful, the building is scholarly in its references, particularly to classical precedent. It occupies the wedge of land at the intersection of Queen Victoria Street and Poultry, a critical City site imbued with the presence of John Soane's Bank of England (1788-1808, listed

Grade I), the Mansion House of 1739-53 by George Dance the Elder (listed Grade I), Sir Edwin Lutyens' Midland Bank Head Office (1924-39, listed Grade I), and Sir Edwin Cooper's National Westminster Bank (1930-32, listed Grade II), and close to Hawksmoor's St Mary Woolnoth (1716-27, listed Grade I), the latter a particular favourite of Stirling. Stirling regarded the site as being very special "at this spider's web intersection surrounded by all those heroes like Lutyens and Hawksmoor and Dance. It's the quintessence of London" (*Sunday Times*, 24 April 1991).

Comparing No.1 Poultry with Lutyens' Midland Bank, Colin St John Wilson observed that "common to both buildings are an element of wit, of knowingness, of 'the high game'; a tradition passed with gathering momentum from generation to generation." (*Architecture Today*, 1998, 60-63). It is planned with geometric precision, a "play of forms that was inventive with a refreshing wit" (*Architecture Today*, 59). Like much of Stirling's late work, such as the Neue Staatsgalerie in Stuttgart, Germany (1979-84) and the Braun headquarters at Melsungen, Germany (1986-92), it is a large building whose bulk is broken down into contrasting volumes and materials that can be readily taken in from a single viewpoint and in progression through the building.

Inevitably for a high profile building in a highly sensitive location, No.1 Poultry received mixed acclaim, conservationists considering it a poor replacement for the destroyed listed buildings, some critics regretting the change in direction Stirling's work was taking, while others have speculated how the building would have appeared had he lived. Following the grant of planning permission and listed building consent, minor revisions to the design were approved in 1995 and 1996. These were designed to meet current safety standards and market conditions at that time, and care was taken to avoid diluting or substantially altering the scheme approved by the Secretary of State in 1989. Revisions included increasing the floor area of the retail space and reducing the number of units; changes to the position of shop entrances and to the public throughway (Bucklersbury Passage); the public roof garden was also designed at that time. No.1 Poultry ranks as one of the major British urban landmarks of the later C20, the building, and debate, illustrating core values of post-modern urbanism, notably that of contextualism, in acknowledging the adjacent buildings in scale and material, and in showing that contrast is essential for meaning to be communicated. The building was shortlisted for the Royal Fine Art Commission Trust Building of the Year Award 1999 and gained a Civic Trust Award in 2000, while the garden, designed by Arabella Lennox-Boyd, won the Soft Landscape Award 1998. The building was not entered for other awards at the client's request.

Architect - Sir James Stirling (1924-92) was born in Glasgow and studied at Liverpool University before setting up in partnership first with James Gowan (1956-63), and then in 1971 with Michael Wilford. Notable works in Britain include: Langham House Close (1957-58), the Leicester University Engineering building (1961-63), each listed at Grade II*; Andrew Melville Hall, University of St Andrews (completed 1964, listed Grade A); the History Faculty Library, Cambridge (1964-68), and the Florey Building for Queen's College, Oxford (1968-71) each listed at Grade II. An extension to Branksome Conference Centre, Haslemere, Surrey for Olivetti (1971-72, listed Grade II*) represents a turning point in his work in the 1970s from the New Brutalist ethos he had espoused early in his career, towards (although he strongly disliked labels) a post-modernist interpretation of the past, fully realised in Britain in No.1 Poultry. James Stirling has claim to be among the first modern British architects to achieve widespread international standing. He was one of the first post-war British architects to work abroad, when in 1974 he was invited to design a museum in Düsseldorf that led directly to that at Stuttgart. Notable in Europe are: the award winning extension to the Neue Staatsgalerie, Stuttgart (1979-84), generally regarded as his masterpiece, Stuttgart Music School and Theatre Academy (1987), Braun Headquarters at Melsungen, all in Germany; the Electra bookshop for the Venice Biennale, Italy (1989), and in North America, the Fogg Museum extension at Harvard University. He was given the Aalto Award in 1977, the RIBA Gold Medal in 1980, and in 1981 was the first British recipient of the Pritzker Prize, considered the world's leading award to an architect. He was awarded the Japanese culture prize "Praemium Imperiale" in 1990, and his knighthood was announced in 1992, shortly before his death. The Stirling Prize, the UK's most prestigious architecture prize, is named after him.

Subject of a biography by Mark Girouard in 1998, the last few years have seen a revival of interest in the architect's work, marked by the publication of a number of studies by authors including Geoffrey H Baker, Mark Crinson, Amanda Reeser Lawrence and Anthony Vidler.

Details
Speculative offices incorporating retail units, the Green Man public house, a public right of way in Bucklersbury Passage and rooftop restaurant and garden. Designed in 1985-88 by James Stirling, Michael Wilford and Associates for Peter Palumbo's City Acre Property Investment Trust Ltd, and built in 1994-98 by the practice, renamed Michael Wilford and Partners after Stirling's premature death in 1992. Architect-in-charge Laurence Bain. Structural and mechanical engineers - Ove Arup and Partners; Main contractor - John Laing Construction; rooftop landscape - Arabella Lennox-Boyd, restaurant - Conran Design Partnership.

Structure and materials - The structure was determined by the underlying geology and archaeology. The building has a reinforced concrete frame on granite foundations and is clad with alternating bands of rusticated buff and red sandstone (Australian Helidon and Wilderness Red from the Forest of Dean, Glocs.); Rosa Gallura granite detail, cladding and paving, and glazed blue tiles lining the atrium; in the principal public areas fixtures and fittings, including windows, are in bronze; elsewhere window frames are predominantly powder coated aluminium, in places brightly coloured. The ground floor level of the atrium or courtyard is paved in York stone, defining the public realm.

Plan - No.1 Poultry occupies the wedge of land at the intersection of Queen Victoria Street and Poultry. Symmetrical in plan and section, laid out about a central longitudinal axis, it is set out on a 1.5m grid which informs the rhythm and bay divisions of the external and inward facing façades and internal plan. In plan it resembles a wedge pierced with an open cylindrical volume into which is inserted a triangular form. The building is of six storeys plus two basement floors; the ground floor and lower ground floor concourse levels incorporate retail units, including covered shopping, an entrance to Bank underground station and public right of way, namely Bucklerbsury Passage. Floors 1-5 are occupied by offices, with a publicly accessible rooftop restaurant and garden above. On the SW corner is a pub opening from the street and concourse. Cutting through the building, Bucklersbury Passage, expressed as a courtyard with an open rotunda above and below, replaces the historic route of Bucklersbury. The design is characteristic of Stirling's work in its exploration of space and movement through interlocking geometrical forms, and in terms of motifs and materials, as first realised at the Staatsgalerie, Stuttgart. The generosity of the public realm is wholly exceptional for a speculative scheme and the interlocking geometry and use of colour have a powerful intensity that derive from the tight constraints of the site. The project was conceived, revised and executed by the same practice, and in principle executed as stipulated, to Stirling's agreed design, as set out in his Proof of Evidence to the Inquiry. Materials were sourced and technical detail finalised after his death, incorporating later revisions and amendments imposed as the building was under construction, for example to allow emergency access.

Exterior - The long elevations are symmetrical in three main bays with atypical bays at the western end. Each elevation has a colonnaded base, rising through two storeys, either side of a projecting monumental opening with sloping sides. Above, the middle and top sections are trade motifs, organised in a pattern of alternating segmental stone bays into which are set two tiers of windows, and V-shaped glass bays, the bay rhythm and parapet height acknowledging the surrounding buildings. The colonnades are separated from the upper floors by a giant bull-nosed stringcourse of grey granite. Behind the colonnades are bronze, segmental glazed shop fronts and at first floor level, windows which are offset from the colonnade. The Poultry elevation incorporates a terracotta frieze of royal progresses by Joseph Kremer, incorporated from the demol-ished 12-13 Poultry, by Frederick Chancellor. Flanking the Poultry entrance, the address - 1 Poultry - is set into the stone in bronze let-tering. The apex of the building is distinguished by a prominent tower. This rises from the blind flanking walls which are carried for-ward at ground floor level to form a large, round-headed entrance with a revolving door. Above this is an acutely angled V-shaped win-dow - echoing those on the side elevations - and the cylindrical tower itself which incorporates a window in the form of a clock and higher up the cantilevered platforms of the viewing turret. Behind, the flanking walling terminates in a bold prow-like cornice. The tower has been compared with that of the Mappin and Webb build-ing (J and J Belcher, 1870-71) which it replaced but may also allude to Roman rostral columns and a 1974 scheme for a Tuscan tower house by Stirling's former assistant, Léon Krier. The clock window, the design completed after Stirling's death, is said to be based on Stirling's own watch.

Internal Spaces - The public thoroughfare through the side en-trances, the ancient right of way of Bucklersbury Passage, is threaded through a centrally placed open court, articulated on the street elevation by the curved form of the drum at the top. Into this volume is inserted a triangle of offices, the switch indicated by the diagrid ceiling of the covered way, the superimposition of geome-tries, a favourite Stirling device, and wall treatment, echoing the al-ternating bays of the exterior. At street level a central triangular gallery within the compass of the structural piers overlooks the lower level concourse and, as on the upper floors, has a bronze handrail. In each quadrant of the ground floor atrium are shop windows of different heights, the main entrance to the office floors to the west (finalised after Stirling's death), and access to the lower concourse to the east. The clock from the Mappin and Webb building is mounted above the entrance. The lower concourse, also circular on plan was designed to accommodate retail outlets, with a restaurant added after completion. At first floor office level the stone-clad wall of the atrium is blind, while the second floor has deep-set small square lights, as if echoing a classically informed basement storey; the triangular inserts of the projecting upper office floors are clad in blue glazed tiles into which deep-set windows with pink, yellow and blue reveals are set, the whole resembling an intimate domestic street or court, as if the tight City street plan is represented in ascending layers. Paving as elsewhere is of granite slabs.

The approach from the apex into the central drum creates a dramatic and fluid relationship of internal and external spaces, exceptional in a post-modernist commercial building, that conjures up the multi-facetted historic fabric of the City, a recurring theme, of cities within cities, in Stirling's later work. Rising from the principal entrance at the apex of the building to the first floor is a dramatic, monumental stair of inclined granite steps, lined within banded masonry walls and beneath a vaulted roof. At upper levels panels appear to pivot, to accommodate small windows which let in light and provide glimpses from the office floor. From the main entrance within the central court, glass-sided lifts rise to roof level where they emerge beneath a steel canopy (the entrance sequence and lifts all detailed after Stirling's death), which oversails the atrium, which can be viewed from the terrace. The rooftop restaurant, named by Terence Conran the Coq d'Argent (Silver Cockerel), punning on the name of the building and its architect, has bronze doors, fixtures and fittings.

The interior, designed by CD Architects (Conran Design) in 1997, appears to have been partly refitted but is essentially as built. The garden, designed by Arabella Lennox-Boyd, reflects the geometrical form of the building. An open loggia within the banded sandstone lined drum is formed of a sturdy oak pergola on granite plinths, with diagonally set paving that echoes the diagrid, and is backed by luxuriant informal planting. A simple opening in the drum wall opens onto a lawn above the prow of the building (astro-turfed in 2015) flanked by formal rows of box hedging and spherical forms and leads to an enclosed circular platform and viewing turret at the apex, a rare instance of a post-modern garden associated with its parent building. The asymmetrical south-western bay on Queen Victoria Street containing the Green Man pub is treated in the manner of the main elevations and turns abruptly to the largely unseen Sise Lane elevation which is in a simpler palette of materials, of stucco walls and geometrical forms. The west-facing pub window is supported on a striking yellow conical shaft, the latter a reference to Stirling's earlier work. Above, deep-set windows picked out in yellow in pronounced rectangular masonry architraves, contrast with the adjacent section where bands of strip glazing, in an almost moderne spirit, are picked out in blue, with yellow portholes above.

Interior - Granite-lined lift lobbies with sloping sides and deep-set lift openings with bright coloured reveals echo the external openings in their form and use of colour. Ceilings which echo the diagrid are apparent in the office floors; the offices and retail units were intended to be flexibly fitted out and have been refitted*. On the first floor are squinch-like internal openings of the windows lighting the monumental stair. On the second office floor the rear openings of the atrium windows are deeper than on the external face. Aside from a perimeter counter below and adjacent to the window, the Green Man pub has also been refitted. Office partitions, fixtures and fittings*, retail unit and concourse restaurant interiors, fixtures and fittings*, the bar and counter* in the Green Man pub, plant and services* and basement storage* and parking facilities* are not of special interest.

* Pursuant to s.1 (5A) of the Planning (Listed Buildings and Conservation Areas) Act 1990 ('the Act') it is declared that these aforementioned features are not of special architectural or historic interest.

118

[Circling the Square]

Marie Bak Mortensen
Vicky Wilson

When architectural patron and developer Peter, later Lord, Palumbo commissioned Mies van der Rohe in 1962 to build a masterpiece of the Modern Movement, replacing a block of listed high-Victorian offices, the site became the focus of one of the most famous architectural planning controversies. Over the course of three decades, Mies's scheme provoked passionate debate, admiration and resistance among the architectural elite and representatives of the conservation movement. By comparing the design methods of two highly recognised architects of the twentieth century it offers a unique opportunity to trace the continuity in purpose and approach that unites two seemingly dissimilar architectural creations proposed for the same site. With the recent premature listing of Number One Poultry, controversy perseveres into the twenty-first century, prompting important questions about the continuing transformation of cities. By lifting the lid on one of the most fascinating periods in British architectural history, this exhibition offers the opportunity to reflect upon our own time of uncertainty and transition.

1984 and beyond
The year 1984 could be described as a dystopian year for modern architecture. On 30 May, the Prince of Wales delivers a hammer blow to modern architects in a speech at Hampton Court Palace. Accusing the profession of ignoring public taste for more traditional styles, he derogatively describes Mansion House Square as "a giant glass stump better suited to downtown Chicago" and de-

nounces ABK's proposed modernist extension to the National Gallery, leading to its dismissal. The speech is indicative of the changing architectural and political landscape of Britain that has fostered the rise of the conservation movement. In the same month, a Public Inquiry into Mansion House Square begins. Although it had been granted conditional planning permission in 1969 by the City Corporation, it takes eleven years for Palumbo to acquire the thirteen freeholds and 348 leaseholds that make up the site. When the scheme comes before the planners again in 1982 it is rejected. Palumbo appeals and an inquiry is set for May 1984.

Leading the opposition is SAVE Britain's Heritage, deeming Mies's architecture outdated and inappropriate in its historic City context. The major bone of contention, however, is the proposed destruction listed buildings, including the neo-Gothic Mappin & Webb (1870) and the triangular Bank of New Zealand (1873). By May 1985, SAVE is victorious when the final decision is made by Patrick Jenkins, Environment Secretary, against the scheme. Only a few years later, the two sides reconvene when Number One Poultry, unable to escape similar controversy, becomes the subject of its own eighteen-day inquiry in 1988. The turbulent planning process that dominated architectural discussion throughout the 1980s and beyond, exemplifies the complex relationship between politics, patronage, public and press.

Mansion House Square
Mies's approach to design centres on the belief that architecture should reflect the epoch in which it is made. For Mies the defining characteristic of the twentieth century is technology; a building's structure should no longer be hidden behind the "architecture" but becomes architecture itself. Such a design principle, exposing external and internal building components, renders any notion of "style" redundant, inspiring Mies's most famous maxim: "less is more."

The paired-back aesthetic is reflected in the design material, most famously in Mies's carefully composed collages, pencil-drawn perspectives and abstract plans. In his later career, however, Mies suffered badly from arthritis and failing eyesight, whereby study models became the primary design tool. Only when a project had been fully developed in three dimensions under Mies's supervision - moving from smaller scale massing models to detailed full size mock-ups - would working drawings be prepared.

The lack of identifiable design material in Mies's own hand led to doubts about the authenticity of Mansion House Square. While some viewed it as the perfect fulfilment of Mies's tower archetype, others regarded it as an uninspired, conveyor-belt approach to design, forcing a generic template into any context. Indeed, the controlled repertoire of Mies's design language is applied here; a rectangular welded-steel skeleton frame raised on stilts; a fully glazed lobby; a rigid modular bay system that informs the scheme's overall planning and proportions; and a steel and glass façade. This appropriation is emphasised by the reuse of Mansion House Square's tower for another unrealised project, the King Broadcasting Studios in Washington State (1967-69). Yet Mies adjusted his design principles on occasion to contextualise his first ever UK commission.

Number One Poultry
The colour, drama and wit of James Stirling's later buildings leave visitors prone to continuous visual surprises. Stirling's intuitive design approach and diverse output can be viewed in contrast to Mies's systematic and objective principles which resulted in a more homogenous architectural language. However, this does not preclude Stirling from also readapting elements from past projects nor employing a controlled methodology; one that meticulously considers all elements of a design in isolation, creating a system of hierarchies that determines the level of detailing for each of the different parts.

For Stirling, the design process is a reversion of Mies's. Instead of working with an archetype that is subjected to subtle adaptations, the Stirling office would initiate the creative process by drawing a wide variety of options for each element. Stirling acting as the "magpie" would select and edit their ideas to narrow down the pre-ferred design route. A Stirling building is therefore the product of creative team interaction, with Stirling retaining ultimate control over its design evolution.

Number One Poultry retains all the essential programmatic com-ponents of Mansion House Square: the public recreational area, the shopping concourse and the office space. However, Stirling's process reassesses and reworks them into a much more integrated spatial solution. In line with his practice's philosophy, Number One Poultry succeeds in weaving public and private spaces together in a series of interlocking functions and sequences. Furthermore, the detailed analysis of pedestrian circulation reflects Stirling's func-tionalist roots, even though visually the building aligns itself with the postmodern aesthetic.

Mansion House Square

Late 1950s Palumbo plans development after his father, Rudolph Palumbo has acquired a significant number of the free- and leaseholds occupying the site

1962 Palumbo commissions Mies van der Rohe

1963 Lord Holford taken on board as consultant

1964, 1967 Mies visits the site in London

1968 Mansion House scheme presented to City Corporation

1969 Letter of intent received from City Corporation in May, approving the scheme in principle. Planning permission withheld until Palumbo acquires the remainder of the site. In August, Mies dies

1971 Bank designated as a conservation area

1982 Scheme resubmitted for planning and is refused

1984 Public Inquiry after Palumbo appeals the decision

1985 Mansion House Square finally rejected in May by Patrick Jenkins, Secretary of State for the Environment

Number One Poultry

1985 In July, Palumbo commissions James Stirling, Michael Wilford & Associates

1987 Planning is rejected by City Corporation

1988 Second Public Inquiry is held

1989 Secretary of State for the Environment Nicholas Ridley approves the scheme

1990 SAVE Britain's Heritage appeal the decision first in the High Court and again in the Appeal Court, where they succeed in overturning it

1991 House of Lords reinstate planning consent

1992 Stirling dies

1993 A third Public Inquiry takes place after attempt by the scheme's opponents to block consent for road closures

1994 Construction begins

1998 Number One Poultry completed

Number One Poultry Team

Laurence Bain, Paul Barke-Asuni, Russ Bevington, Andrew Birds,
Darren Capel, Ian Clavadetcher, Robert Dinse, Felim Dunne,
Frances Dunne, Brian Frost, Liam Hennesy, David Jennings, Toby Lewis,
Tess Mahoney, Catherine Martin, Chris Mathews, Alison McLellan,
Alan Mee, John Munro, Jess Paul, Richard Porchmouth, Peter Ray,
Brian Reynolds, Leandro Rotundi, Mike Russum, Manuel Schupp,
Jackie Simnett, James Stirling, Simon Usher, Karren Waloschek,
Michael Wilford, Ulrike Wilke, Gary Wyatt.

[devised and edited by Marco Iuliano]